Harold R Foster

Prince Valiant

COMPRISING PAGES 1419 THROUGH 1464

The Battle Of Badon Hill

FANTAGRAPHICS BOOKS

ABOUT THIS EDITION:

Produced in cooperation with the Danish publisher Interpresse and several other publishers around the world, this new edition of PRINCE VALIANT is intended to be the definitive compilation of Hal Foster's masterpiece. In addition to this volume, Fantagraphics has in stock twenty-six more collections of Foster's Prince Valiant work (Vols. 1,7-31). The ultimate goal is to have the entirety of Hal Foster's epic, comprising 40 volumes, in print at once.

ABOUT THE PUBLISHER:

Celebrating its 20th anniversary in 1996, FANTAGRAPHICS BOOKS has dedicated itself to bringing readers the finest in comic book and comic strip material, both new and old. Its "classics" division includes *The Complete E.C. Segar Popeye*, the *Complete Little Nemo in Slumberland* hardcover collection, and *Pogo* and *Little Orphan Annie* reprints. Its "modern" division is responsible for such works as Yellow Kid Award-winner *Love and Rockets* by Los. Bros. Hernandez, Peter Bagge's *Hate*, Daniel Clowes's *Eightball*, Chris Ware's *Acme Novelty Library*, Jim Woodring's *Frank* and American editions of work by Muñoz & Sampayo, Alberto Breccia, and F. Solano Lopez, as well as *The Complete Crumb Comics*.

OTHER VOLUMES IN THIS SERIES:

PRINCE VALIANT, Volume 32
"The Battle of Badon Hill"
comprising pages 1419 (April 19, 1964) through 1464 (February 28, 1965)
Published by Fantagraphics Books, 7563 Lake City Way NE, Seattle, WA 98115
Editorial Co-Ordinator: Helle Nielsen
Colored by Camillo Conti
Cover inked by Gorm Transgaard and colored by Søren Håkansson
Fantagraphics Books staff: Kim Thompson, Jason Waskey, and Christopher Brownrigg
Copyright ©1997 King Features Syndicate, Inc., Bull's, Interpresse, & Fantagraphics Books, Inc.
Printed in Denmark
ISBN 0-930193-38-5
First Printing: Fall, 1997

Our Story: PRINCE ARN SETS OFF ON HIS MISSION TO NORTH WALES, TAKING WITH HIM THE THREE YOUNG KNIGHTS WHO WERE HIS COMPANIONS WHILE SCOUTING THE SAXONS IN WHITE HORSE VALE.

WHILE SIR VALIANT AND SIR GAWAIN, COMPANIONS ONCE MORE, RIDE LIGHT-HEARTEDLY WESTWARD TO CONVINCE THE THREE KINGS OF CORNWALL THAT THEIR PROMISE OF TROOPS SHOULD BE FULFILLED.

MANY A YOUNG KNIGHT IS WENDING HIS WAY TO CAMELOT TO JOIN IN THE EXPECTED FIGHTING, AND EACH, ACCORDING TO CUSTOM, CHALLENGES TO A JOUST. GAWAIN AND VAL KEEP IN PRACTICE AND TEACH SOME LESSONS.

PASSING THE MENDIP HILLS THEY COME TO AVALON, ITS THREE HILLS RISING FROM THE MARSHY LAKE AND THE SUN GLEAMING ON THE WALLS OF THE NEW CATHEDRAL BEING BUILT IN THE LITTLE TOWN OF GLASTONBURY.

VAL AND GAWAIN COME INTO CORNWALL RIDING ACROSS THE HIGH AND DESOLATE MOORS, FOR THERE IS EVER TROUBLE IN CORNWALL. SO THEY ARE NOT SURPRISED WHEN THEY DESCEND TO A RIVER CROSSING TO FIND A TROOP OF SOLDIERS GUARDING THE FORD.

"GOOD DAY TO YOU, BROTHERS," CALLS VAL. "RIDING IN THIS SUN IS THIRSTY WORK THAT CALLS FOR A TANKARD OF ALE AT YONDER TAVERN. WILL YOU JOIN US?" SOON THE STERN GUARDSMEN BECOME MERRY DRINKING COMPANIONS AND TALK FREELY. THEY EVEN FURNISH A GUIDE TO SHOW THE WAY TO THEIR KING.

"SO, EACH OF THE KINGS DISTRUSTS THE OTHERS AND KEEPS A GREAT ARMY AT RUINOUS COST FOR HIS PROTECTION. THEY WILL BE RELUCTANT TO OFFER ANY OF THEIR FORCES TO ARTHUR."

NEXT WEEK—**The Reluctant Kings**

4-19-64

Prince Valiant
IN THE DAYS OF KING ARTHUR
BY HAROLD R. FOSTER

Our Story: PRINCE VALIANT AND SIR GAWAIN COME INTO CORNWALL TO ASK THE THREE KINGS FOR THEIR PROMISED LEVY OF SOLDIERS FOR THE COMING WAR WITH THE SAXON HORDE. THEIR GUIDE LEADS THEM TO CAERLOCH WHERE REIGNS KING GRUNDEMEDE.

THE KING GRANTS AUDIENCE WITH THE TWO KNIGHTS AND LISTENS IN SILENCE AS THEY REQUEST TROOPS AND REMIND HIM OF HIS PROMISE WHEN HE SWORE FEALTY TO ARTHUR YEARS AGO, WHEN ARTHUR SAVED THEM FROM THE NORTHMEN. THEN THE PALE-FACED KING CONSULTS WITH HIS ADVISOR, A TALL, GAUNT, ONE-EYED MAN DRESSED IN THE STYLE OF A MAGICIAN.

"WE WILL SEND TWENTY WELL-ARMED MEN. THAT IS ALL WE CAN SPARE, FOR WE MUST PROTECT OUR COAST FROM THE RAIDING SCOTTI AND OUR BORDERS AGAINST THE THREAT OF INVASION BY THE RUTHLESS SCUM UNDER THAT TYRANT KING ALRICK-THE-FAT."

A SERF BRINGS UP THEIR SADDLEBAGS AND HE IS QUITE TALKATIVE: "THE KING ALWAYS CONFERS WITH GIVRIK, FOR HE IS A GREAT SORCERER. HE IS MASTER OF UNCOMFORTABLE MAGIC; HAS THE GIFT OF SECOND SIGHT AND POSSESSES THE EVIL EYE!"

"TO OFFER TWENTY MEN IS AN INSULT. THE OTHER TWO MONARCHS WILL FOLLOW SUIT. WE MUST HAVE TWO HUNDRED FROM EACH. THAT ONE-EYED MAGICIAN IS THE KEY FIGURE HERE."

ON THEIR WAY TO DINNER GIVRIK INTERCEPTS THEM. "BEWARE OF TRIFLING WITH THE BALANCE OF POWER HERE IN CORNWALL, OR WHAT TERRORS WILL BE YOURS IF YOU INVITE THE EVIL EYE!"

THEN HE RAISES HIS BUSHY EYEBROWS AND REVEALS A HORRID SIGHT.

NEXT WEEK — Merlin's Janitor

1420 © King Features Syndicate, Inc., 1964. World rights reserved. 4/26/64

Our Story: LIKE EVERYONE ELSE SIR GAWAIN IS SUPERSTITIOUS AND BELIEVES IN WITCHES, FAIRIES, GIANTS, DRAGONS AND ALL MANNER OF MAGIC. SO, WHEN ONE-EYED GIVRIK THE SORCERER REVEALS THE EVIL EYE, HE IS FILLED WITH FEAR.

AT DINNER GIVRIK PERFORMS MANY MIRACLES. HE PASSES HIS HAND OVER A CRYSTAL GOBLET OF WATER, AND. LO, IT TURNS TO RED WINE. HIS KNIFE RISES TO HIS HAND OF ITS OWN ACCORD. TO VAL THESE ARE ALL THE CHEAP TRICKS OF FAIRGROUND ENTERTAINERS; TRICKS THAT HIS FRIEND SLITH, THE GRINNING SCOUNDREL, TAUGHT HIM TO DO YEARS AGO.

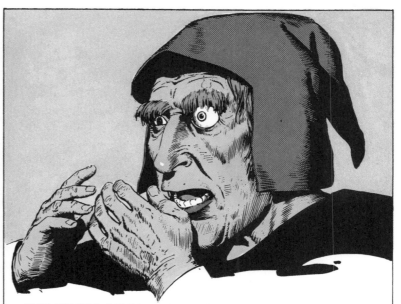

NOW, HIS OLD TEACHER, MERLIN, COULD SHOW THEM SOME REAL MIRACLES..... MERLIN! THE NAME BRINGS BACK MEMORIES. YES! THIS ONE-EYED MOUNTEBANK IS THE LAD WHO LOST AN EYE IN A BARNYARD BRAWL, AND MERLIN, OUT OF PITY, TENDED HIS WOUND AND LET HIM STAY AS A SERVANT.

WHEN THE KING, RATHER TIMIDLY, REQUESTS HIS GREAT WIZARD TO PROPHESY, VAL WATCHES INTENTLY. GIVRIK LOOKS TOWARD THE CEILING, HIS EMPTY EYE SOCKET SHOWING, AS HE MUTTERS WEIRD INCANTATIONS. HE GRIMACES AND MOANS, BUT HIS HANDS ARE FUMBLING IN HIS LAP. THEN HE BURIES HIS FACE IN HIS HANDS, AND WHEN HE LIFTS HIS FACE -- BEHOLD! THE EVIL EYE GLARES FORTH!

VAL HOPES THAT GIVRIK WILL NOT RECOGNIZE IN THE PRINCE AND KNIGHT OF TABLE ROUND, THE YOUNG PUPIL MERLIN TAUGHT SO MANY YEARS AGO.

FROM THE WEAVER'S LOOM, THE KITCHEN AND THE STABLES VAL GATHERS THE ITEMS THAT HE HOPES WILL BREAK THE POWER OF THE COURT WIZARD AND GET THE TROOPS KING ARTHUR SO SORELY NEEDS.

1421

IF THIS GAUNT, GRIM CLOWN CAN INFLUENCE THE COURT WITH THE LITTLE TRICKS HE LEARNED AS MERLIN'S JANITOR, VAL WILL SHOW THEM SOME REAL FAKING.

NEXT WEEK— *Fire from Beyond*

5-3-64

Prince Valiant
IN THE DAYS OF KING ARTHUR
BY HAROLD R FOSTER

Our Story: KING GRUNDEMEDE, ON THE ADVICE OF HIS WIZARD, HAS REFUSED KING ARTHUR THE TROOPS HE PROMISED. BUT WITH A FEW ODDS AND ENDS HE HAS GATHERED, VAL PLANS TO DISCREDIT THE ONE-EYED MAGICIAN.

"GIVRIK, YESTERDAY YOU TURNED WATER INTO WINE, BUT MY POWER IS GREATER—I TURN YOUR WATER TO POISON." WITH A WAVE OF HIS HAND VAL DROPS IN A FEW DYE CRYSTALS, AND BEHOLD!

WITH THE AID OF A FINE HORSEHAIR AND A BIT OF WAX, HE COMMANDS HIS KNIFE TO ARISE AND BREAK UP HIS OATCAKE.

THE PALM OF HIS HAND IS EMPTY AS HE REACHES OUT AND TAKES A GOLD COIN FROM GIVRIK'S EAR.

AGAIN THE INVISIBLE HORSEHAIR AND WAX, AND A FEATHER DANCES TO VAL'S SONG.

NOW COMES THE TEST. IN VAL'S HAND A GLITTERING COIN APPEARS AND DISAPPEARS RAPIDLY. "WATCH IT, WATCH IT!" HE COMMANDS, AND GIVRIK STARES AT IT FASCINATED WHILE VAL PLACES THE END OF A HOLLOW REED IN THE POUCH AND PRESSES THE PLUNGER, SENDING OUT ITS CHARGE OF DRY MUSTARD AND LYE.

"CHARLATAN!" SNEERS VAL, "EVEN YOUR EVIL EYE CANNOT AVAIL AGAINST MY MAGIC." GIVRIK ACCEPTS THE CHALLENGE, FOR HE HAS HAD SUCH SUCCESS WITH THAT TRICK HE ALMOST BELIEVES IT HIMSELF.

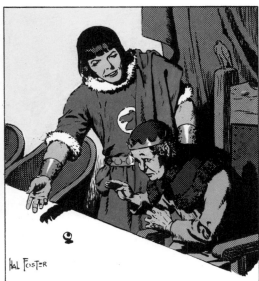

HE GOES THROUGH HIS USUAL GESTURES AND, WHEN HE REMOVES HIS HANDS, THERE IS THE BALEFUL EYE, GLEAMING.

"TOO LONG HAVE YOU USED THE POWER OF DARKNESS. NOW THE DARK GODS WILL CONSUME YOU WITH FLAMES. BURN, GIVRIK, BURN!"

1422

A RETIRED MAGICIAN RUSHES SCREAMING FROM THE ROOM, LEAVING ONLY A PORCELAIN EYE BEHIND.
"NOW, KING GRUNDEMEDE, SHALL WE TALK ABOUT YOUR PROMISED TROOPS?"

NEXT WEEK— *The New Wizard*

5-10-64

Prince Valiant

IN THE DAYS OF KING ARTHUR

BY HAROLD R FOSTER

Our Story: GIVRIK THE WIZARD DEPARTS IN UNSEEMLY HASTE, LEAVING BEHIND ONLY THE PORCELAIN EYE WITH WHICH HE HAS TERRORIZED THE COURT OF KING GRUNDEMEDE. *"HERE IS THE SO-CALLED 'EVIL EYE!'"* AND LAUGHING, PRINCE VALIANT ROLLS IT ACROSS THE TABLE. TO HIS SURPRISE, THE KING RECOILS IN HORROR FROM THE HARMLESS TRINKET.

VAL HAS USED A FEW TRICKS OF PARLOR MAGIC TO CONFOUND THE WIZARD, BUT TO HIS AMAZEMENT, HE FINDS HIMSELF REGARDED AS A GREAT SORCERER. WOULD IT BE FAIR TO CONTINUE THIS DECEPTION TO GET THE TROOPS ARTHUR SO SORELY NEEDS?

"WE CANNOT SPARE YOU THE TWO HUNDRED TROOPS YOU DEMAND. IT WOULD LEAVE US HELPLESS BEFORE THE ARMY OF KING ALRICK-THE-FAT." *"THE NUMBER IS NOW THREE HUNDRED,"* ANSWERS VAL, *"AND AS THEY ARE HIRED MERCENARIES, THEY WILL TURN AGAINST YOU IN REVOLT WHEN YOU CAN NO LONGER PAY THEM."*

"WE WILL MARCH, THREE HUNDRED STRONG, TO THE CASTLE OF ALRICK AND DEMAND A LIKE NUMBER FROM HIM. THUS I WILL SAVE YOU BOTH FROM BANKRUPTCY AND REBELLION."

ALRICK-THE-FAT LOOKS FEARFULLY FROM HIS BATTLE-MENTS AT THE APPROACHING ARMY. HIS OWN RAGTAIL GUARDS HAVE SCUTTLED BEHIND THE WALLS, WHERE THEY ARE SO CROWDED TOGETHER AS TO MAKE THEM USELESS IN CASE OF WAR.
NEXT WEEK—**Obstinate Glutton**

VAL AND GAWAIN START OUT WITH AN UNDISCIPLINED MOB. FOOTSORE, WEARY, BULLIED AND DRILLED, THEY ARRIVE AT THEIR DESTINATION, BUT NOW THERE IS A SEMBLANCE OF UNITY AND EVEN PRIDE.

4123   5-17-64

Prince Valiant
IN THE DAYS OF KING ARTHUR
BY HAROLD R FOSTER

Our Story: PRINCE VALIANT AND SIR GAWAIN BRING THEIR SMALL ARMY BEFORE THE STRONGHOLD OF ALRICK-THE-FAT AND ENCAMP IN STRICT MILITARY FASHION. TO HIS CAPTAINS VAL SAYS: "MAINTAIN A SEVERE DISCIPLINE. THESE RAGGED VAGABONDS MUST LOOK LIKE A FORMIDABLE ARMY FOR A FEW DAYS AT LEAST."

KING ALRICK IS EATING HIS WAY THROUGH THE LONG HOURS BETWEEN MEALS AND LISTENING TO THE SCOLDING OF HIS HANDSOME, COLD-EYED QUEEN. GUARDS HOLD THE TWO VISITORS AT A SAFE DISTANCE, FOR VAL'S FAME AS A MIGHTY WIZARD HAS PRECEDED HIM AND HE IS HELD IN AWE.

ALRICK, BACKED BY HIS GLOWERING SPOUSE, FLATLY REFUSES TO WEAKEN HIS FORCES. EVEN NOW, HIS AGENTS ARE TRYING TO GET SOME OF VAL'S TROOPS TO DESERT TO HIM WITH PROMISES OF BETTER PAY.

"THERE IS BUT ONE THING TO DO: GET THE THREE KINGS OF CORNWALL TO MEET TOGETHER AND SIGN A TRUCE UNTIL THE SAXON WAR IS WON. I RIDE WEST TO FETCH KING HARLOCH."

VAL RIDES WESTWARD ALONE, WHILE A MESSENGER GOES EASTWARD TO FETCH KING GRUNDEMEDE.

5/24/64

AND SIR GAWAIN, ALL BRUSHED, CURLED AND WAXED, MAKES HIS INDOLENT WAY TO THE SOLAR WHERE ALRICK'S QUEEN IS AT HER TAPESTRY.

IT IS NOT OFTEN THAT A HANDSOME KNIGHT VISITS THE COURT, AND SHE IS SO PLEASED THAT SHE ALMOST SMILES.

NEXT WEEK— **The Charmer**

Prince Valiant

IN THE DAYS OF KING ARTHUR

BY HAROLD R. FOSTER

Our Story: THERE ARE THREE KINGS OF CORNWALL. EACH FEARS THE OTHERS, AND TWO OF THEM HAVE RAISED SUCH HUGE ARMIES FOR DEFENSE THAT THEY ARE BANKRUPT. PRINCE VALIANT RIDES WESTWARD TO MEET THE THIRD.

VAL CASTS PRACTICED EYES ABOUT THE COURTYARD AND NODS APPROVAL; EFFICIENT DEFENSES, A SMALL GARRISON OF PROUD WARRIORS. KING HARLOCH MUST BE OF A DIFFERENT STRIPE FROM THOSE OTHER FRIGHTENED KINGS.

THE YEARS HAVE BENT THE BROAD SHOULDERS AND ROBBED HIS GREAT HANDS OF STRENGTH, BUT THE KING SAYS: "I KNOW OF YOUR MISSION, SIR VALIANT, AND WILL HONOR OUR PROMISE TO KING ARTHUR. MY SON, PRINCE CHARLES, WILL LEAD OUR LEVY."

"WE CANNOT OFFER MUCH IN NUMBER, BUT OURS ARE PICKED WARRIORS, STAUNCH IN BATTLE, WHO TWICE HAVE SCATTERED THE MERCENARY MOB KING ALRICK CALLS HIS 'ARMY'!"

MEANWHILE, SIR GAWAIN BEGINS HIS DAY'S WORK: "HOW IS IT, FAIR LADY, THAT YOU HAVE NEVER GRACED THE MERRY HALLS OF CAMELOT? I CAN PICTURE YOU GOWNED IN SHIMMERING CRIMSON, ORNAMENTS OF SILVER, A SINGLE ROSE IN YOUR HAIR, EARNING THE ADMIRATION OF GALLANT KNIGHTS AND THE ENVY OF FAIR WOMEN!"

"MY HUSBAND, KING ALRICK-THE-FAT, CANNOT TRAVEL, AND HAS SPENT HIS LAST PENNY MAINTAINING HIS HUGE ARMY OF UNWASHED VAGABONDS." AND SHE SIGHS.

5-31-64

"THEN GET RID OF THIS UNWANTED ARMY. LET ARTHUR PAY THEM INSTEAD. THEN YOU CAN AFFORD TO FOLLOW AND BE IN TIME FOR THE VICTORY CELEBRATION! CAMELOT WILL BE ABLAZE WITH LIGHT, THERE WILL BE FEASTING AND ENTERTAINMENT AND DANCING UNTIL THE DAWN!"

"YOU ARE A CHARMING LIAR, SIR GAWAIN. YOU DO NOT DECEIVE ME A BIT. I AM PLAIN AND RATHER DULL AND WILL NOT TROUBLE THE HEARTS OF GREAT WARRIORS."
THEN, FOR THE FIRST TIME IN YEARS, THE QUEEN LAUGHS: "BUT YOU HAVE WON, SIR, AND I WILL HELP YOU IF I CAN."

NEXT WEEK- *Tough Meat and Watered Wine*

Prince Valiant

IN THE DAYS OF KING ARTHUR

BY HAROLD R FOSTER

Our Story: SIR GAWAIN WAS NEVER MORE FASCINATING THAN WHEN HE WINS ALRICK'S QUEEN OVER TO HIS PLANS WITH FLATTERY AND PROMISES.

UP FROM THE WEST RIDES A HAPPY PRINCE VALIANT. KING HARLOCH'S LEVY ARE WELL-TRAINED VETERANS WHO WILL OFFICER THE RABBLE ARMY VAL WILL BRING TO CAMELOT, AND PRINCE CHARLES IS A CAPABLE LEADER.

AND FROM THE EAST, KING GRUNDEMEDE BOUNCES ALONG IN A HORSE LITTER, FEARFUL AND BEWILDERED.

THEY ALL COME TOGETHER IN THE HALL OF KING ALRICK-THE-FAT, WHO HAS REFUSED STEADFASTLY TO SEND THE PROMISED LEVY OF MEN TO AID KING ARTHUR. AND ALRICK IS IN A FOUL MOOD. HIS BETWEEN-MEAL SNACK IS OF WATERED WINE, TOUGH MEAT, UNSWEETENED CAKES.

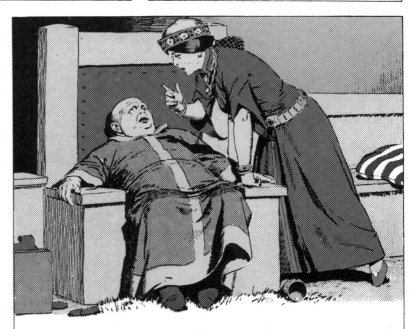

"THE FARE IS POOR," SNAPS HIS QUEEN, "AND IT WILL GET WORSE! IF YOUR FOOD IS MISERABLE, THINK WHAT YOUR ARMY MUST GET. ALREADY THEY GRUMBLE, AND REVOLT IS NEAR. WE FACE POVERTY AND FAMINE."

"NOW, WHAT COULD HAVE BROUGHT THE QUEEN OVER TO OUR SIDE?" VAL WONDERS ALOUD.
"MY DIPLOMACY, OF COURSE," SIMPERS GAWAIN. "WHAT LADY CAN RESIST MY PERSUASION?"

1426   © King Features Syndicate, Inc., 1964. World rights reserved.   6-7-64

BUT THE QUEEN IS NOT FINISHED YET-- "AND GET THOSE UNWASHED RASCALS OUT OF OUR CASTLE. LET ARTHUR PAY AND FEED THEM!" SHE RAGES. "I RIDE TO CAMELOT FOR A VACATION. LET ME KNOW WHEN MY HOME IS FUMIGATED!"

ALRICK SITS PONDERING WHILE ONE BY ONE THE CANDLES SPUTTER AND BURN OUT. HE HAS DREAMED OF TAKING ALL CORNWALL WITH A HUGE ARMY, BUT NOW IT IS HE WHO FEARS HIS OWN ARMY MOST.

NEXT WEEK- *Always a Tomorrow*

Our Story: "BY THE AUTHORITY INVESTED IN ME BY KING ARTHUR, I HAVE DRAWN UP A TREATY. PEACE IS TO BE MAINTAINED IN CORNWALL UNTIL THE SAXON WAR IS OVER, OR THE KING'S ANGER WILL BE AROUSED."

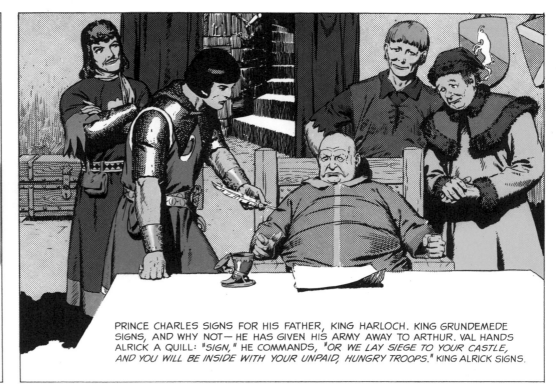

PRINCE CHARLES SIGNS FOR HIS FATHER, KING HARLOCH. KING GRUNDEMEDE SIGNS, AND WHY NOT— HE HAS GIVEN HIS ARMY AWAY TO ARTHUR. VAL HANDS ALRICK A QUILL: "SIGN," HE COMMANDS, "OR WE LAY SIEGE TO YOUR CASTLE, AND YOU WILL BE INSIDE WITH YOUR UNPAID, HUNGRY TROOPS." KING ALRICK SIGNS.

PRINCE VALIANT HAS SUCCEEDED IN RAISING AN ARMY IN CORNWALL.... BUT WHAT AN ARMY. GAWAIN, CHARLES AND A SMALL GROUP OF VETERAN WARRIORS MUST WHIP THESE VAGABONDS INTO SHAPE BEFORE THEY REACH CAMELOT.

THE STRAGGLING MOB COVERS ONLY FIVE MILES THE FIRST DAY. AT THIS RATE THEY MAY REACH CAMELOT TOO LATE. VAL CALLS HIS OFFICERS TOGETHER: "KING ARTHUR HAS SENT SUPPLIES. I HAVE ORDERED THE WAGONS PLACED TWENTY MILES APART. TELL YOUR MEN IT IS TWENTY MILES A DAY OR GO HUNGRY." THE ARMY MOVES MORE QUICKLY.

NOW OUR STORY TURNS TO PRINCE ARN, WHO HAS BEEN SENT INTO NORTH WALES TO PLEAD WITH HIS FRIEND, THE YOUNG KING CUDDOCK, FOR TROOPS TO AID ARTHUR.

1427

6-14

BUT THE BOY-KING IS NOT IN HIS STRONG-HOLD. A RAID BY THE SCOTTI HAS CALLED HIM AWAY TO THE COAST. ARN FOLLOWS.

THE SCOTTI HAVE STRUCK AND GONE AND, AS USUAL, NOT A LIVING THING STIRS AMONG THE SMOLDERING RUIN.

NEXT WEEK— *Grim Tidings*

Our Story: PRINCE ARN FINDS YOUNG KING CUDDOCK SURVEYING THE AWFUL RESULT OF A SCOTTI RAID. *"THEIR RAIDS HAVE INCREASED TENFOLD. HARDLY A DAY GOES BY BUT OUR LOOKOUTS REPORT THEIR SHIPS OFF OUR COASTS. THEY STRIKE AND RUN, AND IT WILL TAKE AN ARMY TO PROTECT OUR SHORES."*

WHILE THE BURIAL PARTY IS AT WORK ARN MAKES A DISCOVERY. A SAXON HELMET! CAN THIS MEAN THE SAXONS ARE ENCOURAGING THE STEPPED-UP RAIDS?

ONE OF THE YOUNG KNIGHTS OF ARN'S ESCORT HAS A SUGGESTION: *"WHY REBUILD THE VILLAGE AND TEMPT ANOTHER RAID? RATHER PUT FUEL IN THE RUINED HOUSES TO BE LIT WHEN RAIDERS APPEAR. THEY WILL NOT ATTACK A SMOLDERING RUIN."*

FORTS AND WATCHTOWERS ARE BUILT TO KEEP THE SCOTTI FROM COMING INLAND. BUT ALL THIS IS TAKING VALUABLE TIME, AND ARN IS IN DESPAIR OF GETTING THE WELSH TROOPS KING ARTHUR SO SORELY NEEDS.

A MESSENGER ARRIVES FROM CAMELOT. THE SAXON ARMY IS ON THE MOVE, A MIGHTY HOST! ARN IS TO BRING WHATEVER TROOPS HE CAN GATHER, IMMEDIATELY.

1428   © King Features Syndicate, Inc., 1964. World rights reserved.   6-21

THE BOY-KING GATHERS HIS ADVISORS TOGETHER AND SAYS: *"WE BELIEVE THE SAXONS ARE AIDING THE SCOTTI RAIDERS, SO WE CANNOT GIVE AID TO ARTHUR. HOWEVER, IF HE IS DEFEATED, WE DIE OR BECOME SAXON SLAVES! WHAT DO YOU ADVISE?"*

NEXT WEEK— *The Horses*

Prince Valiant

IN THE DAYS OF KING ARTHUR

BY HAROLD R FOSTER

Our Story: PRINCE ARN, WITH HIS USUAL GRAVE COURTESY, LEAVES THE COUNCIL CHAMBER, THAT KING CUDDOCK AND HIS ADVISORS CAN TALK FRANKLY AND DECIDE WHETHER TO DEFEND THEMSELVES AGAINST THE SCOTTI RAIDS OR HELP KING ARTHUR.

"THE RAIDS ARE BECOMING MORE SEVERE AND WE MUST PROTECT OUR HOMELAND, BUT THE COUNCIL HAS DECIDED TO OFFER WHAT SMALL AID WE CAN TO ARTHUR."

THE DAYS DRAG ON AND ARN IS IN DESPAIR. HOW CAN HE MARCH THE LONG MILES AND REACH THE BATTLEFIELD IN TIME? THEN DESPAIR TURNS TO JOY.

FROM THE GREEN HILLS AND LUSH MEADOWS COME THE HORSES THAT ARE THE PRIDE OF THE KINGDOM, SURE-FOOTED, SWIFT AND WELL-TRAINED!

"THE WARRIORS ARE FINE HORSEMEN AND EACH WILL LEAD TWO SPARE MOUNTS. MAYBE WE CAN FILL THESE SADDLES WITH RECRUITS ON OUR WAY, FOR I RIDE WITH YOU TO MY FIRST BATTLE!"

SWIFT AS THEY RIDE, THE DAYS SEEM TO PASS EVEN MORE QUICKLY. THE YOUNG KING FEARS HE WILL ARRIVE TOO LATE FOR HIS FIRST TASTE OF WAR.

IT IS ABOUT THIS TIME THAT PRINCE VALIANT ARRIVES AT CAMELOT WITH THE CORNWALL LEVY. "GAWAIN, VAL!" CRIES ARTHUR, "WE FEARED YOU WOULD NOT ARRIVE IN TIME. THE SAXON HOST IS ON THE MARCH AND THEIR NUMBERS ARE AS THE SANDS OF THE SHORE. WE ARE READY TO RIDE TO OUR CHOSEN BATTLEGROUND."

NEXT WEEK— *Marching Armies*

HAL FOSTER

1429

6-28

Prince Valiant
IN THE DAYS OF KING ARTHUR
BY HAROLD R FOSTER

Our Story: HENGIST BEGINS HIS MARCH AND THE VERY GROUND TREMBLES UNDER THE TREAD OF HIS MIGHTY ARMY. NO PLUNDERING RAID THIS, BUT A SUPREME EFFORT TO CONQUER BRITAIN. FAIR LANDS STRETCH BEFORE THEM, A BLACKENED DESERT BEHIND.
FOR A YEAR HENGIST HAS BEEN PLANNING, GATHERING IN THE WAR BANDS AND SPYING OUT HIS ROUTE. IN THIS HE HAS BEEN LUCKY. A VIKING LAD HAS SHOWN HIS SCOUTS THE PERFECT WAY INTO THE COUNTRY'S HEART-LAND.

AND THAT VIKING LAD HAD BEEN ARN, SON OF SIR VALIANT. HE HAD SHOWN THE SAXONS THE ROUTE UP THE THAMES VALLEY AND THROUGH THE WHITE HORSE VALE. NOW THAT KING ARTHUR KNOWS WHERE TO EXPECT THE ATTACK, HE CAN CHOOSE AND PREPARE HIS OWN BATTLEGROUND.

NOW ARTHUR FASTENS HIS SWORD, EXCALIBUR, TO HIS BELT AND MOUNTS HIS GREAT WAR HORSE. THE TIME HAS COME TO PIT HIS SMALL ARMY OF PROUD WARRIORS AGAINST THE SAVAGE HORDE OF SAXONS.

AND THE SITE HE HAS CHOSEN TO DO BATTLE IS BADON HILL, WHERE PRINCE ARN HAD HIS ADVENTURE WITH THE SAXON SCOUTS. HERE ARTHUR AND HIS CHIEFTAINS PLAN THEIR STRATEGY AND PREPARE THE FIELD.

1430

7-5-64

FROM NORTH WALES, RIDING HARD, COME ARN AND YOUNG KING CUDDOCK WITH A TROOP OF HORSEMEN HOPING TO ARRIVE IN TIME, FOR ARTHUR WILL NEED EVERY SWORD AND SPEAR.
NEXT WEEK- **The Last Reserves**

Our Story: THE SETTING SUN GLEAMS ON HORNED HELMETS AND SPEAR POINTS AS THE SAXON HORDE AT LAST APPEARS, FILLING THE VALE WITH ITS VAST NUMBERS. AS NIGHT FALLS, A THOUSAND CAMPFIRES FLICKER IN THE DARKNESS. SUCH A HOST HAS NEVER BEFORE MARCHED ON BRITAIN.

AT DAWN BATTLE LINES ARE FORMED, AND HENGIST, KNOWING HE CANNOT HOLD BACK HIS SAVAGE WARRIORS, SENDS THEM SHOUTING TOWARDS THEIR WAITING FOES.

ARTHUR'S FOOT SOLDIERS FORM IN THREE LINES ACROSS THE VALLEY FLOOR. EVERY QUARTER-HOUR A TRUMPET SOUNDS AND THE FIRST LINE STEPS BACK AND THE LINE BEHIND TAKES ITS PLACE. THE SAXONS, HAMPERED BY THEIR OWN NUMBERS, MUST ALWAYS FACE FRESH TROOPS.

"SIR VALIANT, THE RIGHT WING IS GIVING WAY. TAKE YOUR TROOP AND RELIEVE THE PRESSURE!"
"GAWAIN, THE SAXONS ARE SWARMING OUT OF THE VALE AND WILL GET TO OUR REAR. DRIVE THEM BACK!"

"AND NOW, LANCELOT, IT IS OUR TURN. SEE, THE HORSETAIL STANDARD OF HENGIST IS ADVANCING TOWARD OUR STANDARD. HE WANTS TO CONTEND WITH ME PERSONALLY AND SHOULD NOT BE KEPT WAITING."

ALL OF ARTHUR'S FORCES ARE NOW COMMITTED TO THE BATTLE AND IT IS WIN OR DIE, FOR THERE ARE NO RESERVES TO CALL ON.... UNLESS....

.....THE SMALL TROOP PRINCE ARN BROUGHT FROM WALES CAN BE COUNTED UPON. AND THEY ARE STILL FAR AWAY, BUT RACING TOWARD THE DISTANT ROAR OF BATTLE.

NEXT WEEK— **The Gamble**

1431   7-12-64

Prince Valiant
IN THE DAYS OF KING ARTHUR
BY HAROLD R. FOSTER

Our Story: THE BATTLE OF BADON HILL ROARS TO ITS PEAK AND THE FATE OF A NATION HANGS IN THE BALANCE. PRINCE VALIANT FEELS AGAIN THE SAVAGE ECSTASY OF COMBAT AS HE LEADS HIS TROOP AGAINST THE SAXONS WHO ARE ENCIRCLING THE RIGHT WING.

SIR GAWAIN LEADS A CHARGE THAT FORCES THE SAVAGE FOE BACK INTO THE VALE WHERE THE NUMBERS ARE SO GREAT THAT MOST OF THEM HAVE NOT BEEN ABLE TO REACH THE FIGHTING FRONT.

THE HORSETAIL STANDARD OF HENGIST NEARS THE STANDARD OF ARTHUR PENDRAGON, AND MIGHTY DEEDS ARE DONE WHEN THE HARDIEST WARRIORS OF BOTH SIDES CONTEND FOR VICTORY.

ALL THIS MEETS THE EYE OF PRINCE ARN AS HE ARRIVES AT THE EDGE OF THE VALE. THE YOUNG KING CUDDOCK IS STUNNED AT THE MAGNITUDE OF THE CONFLICT. "ARN, WHAT CAN OUR SMALL TROOP DO AGAINST SUCH NUMBERS?" HE CRIES. "IT WAS ONLY A SMALL STONE THAT BROUGHT GOLIATH DOWN," ANSWERS ARN.

THE FOOT SOLDIERS ARE STILL HOLDING THE SHIELD-WALL ACROSS THE VALLEY FLOOR, BUT NOW THEIR THREE LINES ARE REDUCED TO TWO. STEP BY STEP THEY RETREAT, LEAVING THE DEAD AND WOUNDED TO HAMPER THE STEPS OF THE SAXONS. NOW THE SAXONS SPREAD OUT AND THREATEN TO ENGULF THE LEFT WING.

"THERE IS OUR TARGET!" SHOUTS ARN, POINTING. CHARGING DOWNHILL, KING CUDDOCK IS IN THE MIDST OF HIS FIRST BATTLE.

"SIRE, THE LINE IS CRUMBLING UNDER THE PRESSURE OF NUMBERS," BELLOWS LANCELOT. "SO I SEE," ANSWERS ARTHUR. "SOUND THE TRUMPETS AND CALL ALL THE MOUNTED KNIGHTS TO OUR STANDARD. WE MUST GAMBLE ALL ON ONE CAST OF THE DICE."

NEXT WEEK - *The Seeds of Panic*

1432   7-19-64

Prince Valiant

IN THE DAYS OF KING ARTHUR
BY HAROLD R FOSTER

Our Story: KING ARTHUR SIGNALS HIS TRUMPETER, AND THE RALLYING CALL RINGS OUT, BRINGING THE SURVIVING KNIGHTS TO THE STANDARD.

HENGIST, SURROUNDED BY HIS EARLS AND FIERCEST WARRIORS, REACHES THE TOP OF BADON HILL WHERE ARTHUR AND HIS PICKED KNIGHTS AWAIT HIM. POETS AND TROUBADORS STILL TELL OF THE MIGHTY DEEDS THAT TOOK PLACE THAT DAY.

FROM THE HILLTOP HENGIST LOOKS DOWN. ALTHOUGH HIS WARRIORS OUTNUMBER ARTHUR'S TWENTY TO ONE, THEY ARE BEING CONTAINED ON THE VALLEY FLOOR IN A STRUGGLING MASS. ONLY THE FRONT LINE CAN STRIKE A BLOW!

PRINCE VALIANT AND HIS COMPANIONS-AT-ARMS HAVE SAVED THE RIGHT WING, WHEN THE TRUMPET CALLS THEM TO THE STANDARD. BUT WHAT OF THE LEFT WING? HE GLANCES BACK. A TROOP OF WILD-RIDING HORSEMEN COME STORMING DOWN THE SLOPE AND SCATTER THE ENVELOPING SAXONS. WHO ARE THEY?

HENGIST MUST GET HIS WARRIORS OUT OF THE VALE AND BEHIND THE SHIELD WALL. HIS MEN SEE THE HORSETAIL STANDARD RACING DOWN THE HILL. CAN THIS MEAN A RETREAT, ARE THEY LOSING THE BATTLE?

THEN THE KNIGHTS OF THE ROUND TABLE COME POURING OVER THE CREST OF BADON HILL IN A GLITTERING FLOOD. INTO THE TIGHTLY-PACKED SAXONS THEY CRASH AT AN ANGLE, SLICING OFF SMALL SECTIONS.

1433

7-26-64

AND THESE GROUPS, TOO SMALL TO CONTEND WITH MOUNTED KNIGHTS, RUN FOR SAFETY. THE SEEDS OF PANIC ARE SOWN.

NEXT WEEK— *Victory at Badon Hill*

Prince Valiant
IN THE DAYS OF KING ARTHUR

HAROLD R FOSTER

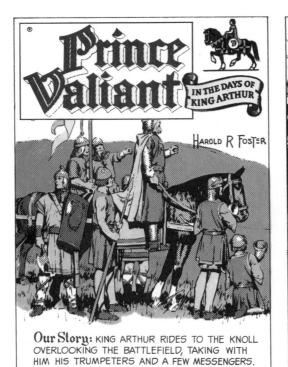

Our Story: KING ARTHUR RIDES TO THE KNOLL OVERLOOKING THE BATTLEFIELD, TAKING WITH HIM HIS TRUMPETERS AND A FEW MESSENGERS. FROM THERE HE DIRECTS THE BATTLE.

THE MIGHTY KNIGHTS OF THE ROUND TABLE FORM THE TERRIBLE WEDGE AND, LIKE A PLOWSHARE, CUT A CRIMSON PATH THROUGH THE PRESS, LOPPING OFF SMALL DETACHMENTS.

IT IS PRINCE VALIANT'S TASK TO CHARGE THESE GROUPS AND SCATTER THEM IN PANIC.

THE VAST MAJORITY OF THE SAXON HORDE HAVE STRUGGLED ALL DAY TO REACH THE FIGHTING FRONT. CRUSHED TOGETHER, UNABLE TO MOVE, THEY WATCH AS THE KNIGHTS SLICE EVER CLOSER AS ONE WOULD PEEL AN ONION. PANIC BEGINS TO SWEEP THROUGH THEM.

AND PANIC IS A STRANGE MADNESS. BOLD WARRIORS WHO WOULD FACE DEATH IN BATTLE WITHOUT FEAR DROP THEIR WEAPONS AND RUN LIKE FRIGHTENED RABBITS.

TWO YOUNG WARRIORS LEAVE THE FIELD. BOTH ARE BLEEDING FREELY FROM VERY SATISFACTORY BATTLE WOUNDS. HOW PROUD THEY ARE!

HAL FOSTER

HENGIST MIGHT HAVE RE-FORMED FOR A COUNTERATTACK, BUT THE CAMP FOLLOWERS, COOKS, SERVANTS AND SLAVES HAD ARRANGED THE BAGGAGE WAGONS ACROSS THE VALLEY FLOOR SO THEY COULD VIEW THE GREAT BATTLE. NOW IT IS LIKE A DAM HOLDING BACK THE FLOOD OF FUGITIVES.

NEXT WEEK— **The Wagon Train**

Prince Valiant
IN THE DAYS OF KING ARTHUR
BY Harold R Foster

Our Story: WHEN VICTORY IS WON THE GREAT CAPTAINS JOIN ARTHUR UNDER HIS STANDARD. THE DESTRUCTION OF A BEATEN ENEMY USUALLY IS LEFT TO LESSER KNIGHTS AND FOOT SOLDIERS. BUT THIS TIME ARTHUR SAYS: *"WE HAVE TREATED THE SAXON FAIRLY, ALLOWING HIM TO MAKE A HOME ON OUR SOIL, ONLY TO HAVE HIM TURN UPON US AT EVERY OPPORTUNITY. LET US FINISH OUR WORK!"*

AND SO THE PURSUIT CONTINUES AT THE WAGONS, AT RIVER CROSSINGS AND BEYOND. THOSE WHO ESCAPE THE SWORD FALL FROM HUNGER, FOR THEY HAD LAID WASTE THE COUNTRYSIDE IN THEIR ADVANCE.

"WE HAVE REACHED THE SEA, NO SAXON STANDS BEFORE US, OUR WORK IS FINISHED," ANNOUNCES ARTHUR. HENGIST HAS SOMEHOW MANAGED TO ESCAPE, BUT NOW HIS POWER IS BROKEN, AND THIRTY YEARS WILL PASS BEFORE THE SAXONS MOUNT ANOTHER INVASION.

SEVERAL YOUNG WARRIORS WHO HAVE WON HONOR ON THE FIELD OF BATTLE ARE KNIGHTED. AND ONE OF THEM IS PRINCE CHARLES WHO LED THE ARMY FROM CORNWALL.

TO BE A PRINCE AND HEIR TO A KINGDOM IS AN HONOR, BUT TO BE ONE OF ARTHUR'S KNIGHTS IS GREATER. AND MAYBE SOME-DAY HE MIGHT GAIN A SEAT AT TABLE ROUND.

TWO WOUNDED VETERANS OF THE LATE WAR HAVE BEEN BROUGHT BACK TO CAMELOT AND RECEIVE VERY SPECIAL ATTENTION. YOUNG KING CUDDOCK HAS THE DUBIOUS HONOR OF WINNING THE AFFEC-TIONS OF THE TWINS, AND THIS COULD LEAD TO A MINOR DISASTER.
NEXT WEEK — *Rivals*

1435   8-9-64

Prince Valiant

IN THE DAYS OF KING ARTHUR

BY HAROLD R FOSTER

Our Story: THE BATTLE OF BADON HILL HAS BEEN A GREAT VICTORY AND ALL BRITAIN IS ASSURED OF PEACE FOR YEARS TO COME. THE BOISTEROUS VICTORS RETURN TO CAMELOT FOR FEASTING AND CELEBRATION, AND PROUDEST OF ALL IS PRINCE CHARLES, WHOSE LEADERSHIP OF THE CORNWALL LEVY HAS WON HIM KNIGHTHOOD.

THE PRICE OF VICTORY COMES HIGH, AND MANY A NEW-MADE WIDOW HAS NO HEART FOR THE GAIETY OF THE COURT.

PRINCE VALIANT BRINGS SIR CHARLES HOME WITH HIM AND FINDS ALETA BUSY NURSING TWO VETERAN WARRIORS WHO HAVE RECEIVED WAR WOUNDS. SHE IS ALSO ENTERTAINING AILIANORA.

THE FIRST PERSON SIR GAWAIN MEETS IS GAYLE, WIFE OF KING ALRICK-THE-FAT. "YOU *WHEEDLED ME WITH SWEET LIES INTO HELPING YOU RAISE AN ARMY IN CORNWALL AND PROMISED I WOULD BE QUEEN OF BEAUTY IN CAMELOT. WELL, I'VE COME, AND MY NIECE GRACE WILL PROVIDE THE BEAUTY I LACK.*"

NO MARRIED WOMAN CAN STAND SEEING A HAPPY BACHELOR WHEN THERE ARE SINGLE GIRLS AROUND. WHEN THE LADY GAYLE SEES CHARLES SHE KNOWS WHERE HER DUTY LIES.

AILIANORA IS A TALL, FAIR GIRL, DESERVING OF A HANDSOME HUSBAND. AFTER LOOKING OVER THE FIELD ALETA DECIDES SIR CHARLES IS MOST SUITABLE. ALAS, CHARLES, YOUR DAYS OF BACHELORHOOD ARE NUMBERED.

1436   © King Features Syndicate, Inc., 1964. World rights reserved.   8-16-64

THE TWINS, KAREN AND VALETA, HAVE NEVER SEEN ANYTHING AS BEAUTIFUL AS CUDDOCK, YOUNG KING OF NORTH WALES. AND HE WHO HAS BRAVELY FACED THE SAXONS QUAILS BEFORE THEIR DETERMINED CAMPAIGN.

NEXT WEEK—*The Matchmaker*

Our Story: THE LADY ALETA IS TAKING HER PROTEGE, AILIANORA, TO THE PALACE WHEN A STRANGE THING HAPPENS. SIR CHARLES IS WALKING BENEATH THE GARDEN WALL AND GAYLE, A QUEEN OF CORNWALL, AND HER NIECE ARE WATCHING HIM........

...... QUEEN GAYLE LIFTS A FLOWER POT, TAKES CAREFUL AIM AND DROPS IT ON HIS HEAD. *"YOU MIGHT HAVE HURT HIM,"* PROTESTS GRACE. *"WHY DID YOU DO IT?"*

"TO GET HIS ATTENTION," ANSWERS GAYLE. *"NOW RUN DOWN AND APOLOGIZE, BE VERY FEMININE, SORRY, CHARMING AND JUST A TRIFLE STUPID."*

"OH, SIR CHARLES, HOW CAN YOU EVER FORGIVE POOR CLUMSY LITTLE ME! COME OVER HERE TO THE STEPS SO I CAN BRUSH YOU OFF. YOU ARE SO BIG AND TALL YOU MAKE ME FEEL LIKE A HELPLESS LITTLE CHILD."

"THAT WAS A NASTY PLOT TO GAIN HIS ATTENTION. I SAW IT. BUT IT WILL DO YOU NO GOOD, HE IS GOING TO MARRY AILIANORA," SAYS ALETA.
"AND WILL YOU USE NASTY LITTLE PLOTS TOO?" ASKS GAYLE.
ALETA CONSIDERS. *"YES,"* SHE ADMITS.
"SPOKEN LIKE A WOMAN," LAUGHS GAYLE. *"WE SHOULD HAVE QUITE A CONTEST."*

HER EYELASHES FLUTTER MODESTLY, HER WHITE HANDS ARE SOFT, HER HAIR LUSTROUS, AND SHE SMELLS LIKE SOME SORT OF FLOWER. HE HAS NOT BEEN THIS CLOSE TO A GIRL BEFORE, AND HIS HEAD BEGINS TO SWIM.

NOW THAT THEY KNOW HOW TO GET A MAN'S ATTENTION, THE TWINS AWAIT THE COMING OF CUDDOCK. *"DON'T HIT HIM ON HIS WOUNDED HEAD,"* ADVISES THE GENTLE VALETA. *"THAT'S ALL RIGHT, I'VE REMOVED THE POT,"* ANSWERS THE MATTER-OF-FACT KAREN.

"WE GOT HIS ATTENTION ALL RIGHT, BUT HE DOES NOT SEEM TO LOVE US MORE," MURMURS VALETA.
"SHOULD I THROW THE POT TOO?" KAREN WONDERS.

NEXT WEEK— **The Nymph**

1437   8-23

Prince Valiant

IN THE DAYS OF KING ARTHUR

BY HAROLD R FOSTER

Our Story: QUEEN ALETA SIZES UP HER ENTRY CAREFULLY. AILIANORA IS TALL, BLONDE AND WELL PUT TOGETHER. ATHLETIC PERHAPS, BUT NOT TOO VIVACIOUS. HER OPPONENT, ON THE OTHER HAND, IS SMALL, CUDDLY AND FULL OF GAIETY.

SHE MUST SHOW HER CANDIDATE TO HER BEST ADVANTAGE. SO ALETA TAKES THE PUZZLED AILIANORA TO THE LILY POND TO AWAIT THE PASSING OF SIR CHARLES.

CHARLES BOWS AS HE PASSES, AND THEN AN ACCIDENT OCCURS. AILIANORA FALLS INTO THE POND!

"HELP! HELP! SIR CHARLES, QUICK, TO THE RESCUE!" CHARLES GALLANTLY HELPS THE DRIPPING GIRL. HER WET HAIR GLEAMS LIKE GOLD IN THE SUNLIGHT AND HER SIMPLE GOWN CLINGS TO HER. HE LOOKS AT HER IN FRANK APPROVAL, FOR HE IS A GOOD JUDGE OF HORSEFLESH AND CAN DISCOVER NO FLAW ANYWHERE IN THIS YOUNG CREATURE.

"NOW COVER HER WITH YOUR CLOAK AND TAKE HER HOME BEFORE SHE CATCHES COLD!" OTHER EYES HAVE WATCHED THE PERFORMANCE.

"THAT WAS A SCURVY TRICK," SCOLDS GAYLE, QUEEN OF CORNWALL. "AN IMMODEST WAY TO SHOW OFF HER NICE FIGURE... I WISH I HAD THOUGHT OF THAT FIRST!"

BELIEVING THEIR ELDERS KNOW ALL THE TRICKS TO WIN A MAN'S LOVE, THE TWINS AWAIT THE PASSING OF YOUNG KING CUDDOCK. VALETA SCREAMS AND TOPPLES INTO THE LILY POND.

HAL FOSTER

"IF I WERE AS CLUMSY AS YOU TWO I WOULD HAVE A NURSEMAID IN ATTENDANCE AT ALL TIMES," GROWLS THE HARRIED LAD AS HE HEAVES VALETA ASHORE.

NEXT WEEK — **The War Is On**

Prince Valiant

IN THE DAYS OF KING ARTHUR

BY Harold R Foster

Our Story: TWO MANAGERS HAVE ENTERED THEIR CONTESTANTS IN THE MATRIMONIAL SWEEPSTAKES, WITH SIR CHARLES AS THE PRIZE. ALETA IS SPONSORING HER PROTEGE, AILIANORA, WHILE QUEEN GAYLE DIRECTS THE DESTINY OF GRACE. AS THIS IS A CONTEST BETWEEN WOMEN, THE RULES OF FAIR PLAY HAVE BEEN SUSPENDED FOR THE DURATION.

ALETA ARRANGES TO HAVE SIR CHARLES TAKE AILIANORA HAWKING. SHE LOOKS BEAUTIFUL, HER CHEEKS FLUSHED, HER EYES BRIGHT WITH EXCITEMENT.

QUEEN GAYLE COUNTERS BY ARRANGING A DANCE IN THE EVENING. GRACE IS FRESH AND GAY, WHILE AILIANORA IS TIRED AND A BIT SORE FROM RIDING.

ALETA REQUESTS SIR CHARLES TO INSTRUCT AILIANORA IN ARCHERY. "I KNOW YOU ARE A GOOD ARCHER," ALETA TELLS THE GIRL, "BUT DO NOT SHOW YOUR SKILL AT FIRST. LET CHARLES BELIEVE HIS INSTRUCTIONS ARE MAKING YOU A FINE BOWMAN."

GAYLE PLAYS HER TRUMP! A PICNIC IN A SUNNY GLADE FAR FROM PRYING EYES... WELL, ALMOST. THE TWINS HAVE WATCHED THEIR ELDERS TRYING TO SNARE THE AFFECTIONS OF SIR CHARLES. SPORT AND FOOD JUST MIGHT WORK ON YOUNG CUDDOCK.

WITH A BRIGHT LURE THEY ATTRACT THE TROUT WITHIN REACH OF HIS SPEAR.

1439   © King Features Syndicate, Inc. 1964. World rights reserved.   9-6

THEN THEY STUFF HIM WITH FOOD, FOR CUDDOCK, YOUNG KING OF NORTH WALES, IS THE MOST GORGEOUS THING THE TWINS HAVE EVER SEEN AND MUST BE MADE TO RETURN THEIR LOVE, WHETHER HE WANTS TO OR NOT.

TWO VICTIMS OF WOMEN'S PLOTTING COMPARE NOTES. "HOW CAN A MAN GET RID OF TWO INSISTENT WOMEN WITHOUT BEING RUDE?" ASKS CUDDOCK.
"OH, IT IS THE PRICE ONE MUST PAY FOR BEING ATTRACTIVE TO THE LADIES," ANSWERS THE BEMUSED CHARLES.

HAL FOSTER

NEXT WEEK—The Ringer

Prince Valiant
IN THE DAYS OF KING ARTHUR
BY HAROLD R FOSTER

Our Story: SIR CHARLES' CONCEIT IS AT HIGH TIDE. IT SEEMS AS IF FAIR LADIES EVERYWHERE ARE VYING FOR HIS FAVOR. DRESSED IN NEW FINERY HE GOES OUT TO GIVE THEM A TREAT. HIS REASONING POWER IS AT LOW EBB.

HE IS BROUGHT DOWN FROM THE CLOUDS BY A DISDAINFUL SNIFF. TURNING, HE SEES A THIN GIRL WITH STRAIGHT RED HAIR AND MANY FRECKLES STARING AT HIM. "NOW, WHAT DID I DO TO DESERVE THAT?" HE DEMANDS.

"BECAUSE YOU ARE SUCH A SIMPLETON AS TO LET TWO DESIGNING WOMEN USE YOU AS A MATRIMONIAL PRIZE FOR THEIR WARDS. IT IS BECAUSE YOU ARE HEIR TO A THRONE, CERTAINLY NOT ON ACCOUNT OF YOUR GOOD LOOKS," SHE SNAPS.

"WHO ARE YOU TO TALK OF GOOD LOOKS?" ROARS CHARLES ANGRILY. "YOU ARE THIN AS A LANCE AND FRECKLED LIKE A RUSTY HELMET!"

"YOKEL," SHE ANSWERS, AS SHE SWINGS DOWN FROM HER PERCH AND WALKS AWAY, PROUDLY ERECT. AFTER ALL THE ATTENTION HE HAS RECEIVED FROM AILIANORA AND GRACE, THIS REBUFF HAS QUITE CUT HIM DOWN TO SIZE, A SMALL SIZE.

THEN HER SHOULDERS SAG. WITH HEAD BOWED SHE STUMBLES AWAY. "WAIT, LADY," HE CALLS, "I DID NOT MEAN TO BE SO RUDE. IF I HURT YOU I AM SORRY!"
"LET ME GO," SHE SOBS.

BUT HE HAS A FIRM GRIP ON HER THIN SHOULDER AND STARES AT THE TEAR-WET, FRECKLED FACE; "BUT WHAT... WHY...?" HE STAMMERS.
"BECAUSE I LOVE YOU. I HAVE LOVED YOU SINCE YOU CAME TO CAMELOT. NOW LET ME GO, YOU HOMELY CLOWN!"

MINUTES GO BY, LONG BREATHLESS MINUTES, WHILE A WONDERFUL TRUTH BECOMES CLEAR. "WE WILL PROBABLY HAVE THE HOMELIEST CHILDREN IN ALL CORNWALL," HE ANNOUNCES. "WHAT IS YOUR NAME?"

NEXT WEEK—The Bride

Our Story: SIR CHARLES, HIS HEAD IN THE CLOUDS, HOLDS HIS NEW-FOUND TREASURE TIGHT IN HIS ARMS. THAT SHE IS THIN, RED-HAIRED AND FRECKLED MAKES NO DIFFERENCE. TO HIM SHE IS THE MOST PRECIOUS THING IN THE WORLD.

"YOU DISAPPOINT ME, SIR CHARLES," SCOLDS ALETA, "MY WARD, AILIANORA, WOULD MAKE A BEAUTIFUL ORNAMENT TO ANY COURT."
"YOU WILL RUE THIS DAY," SAYS QUEEN GAYLE DARKLY, "FOR MY NIECE WOULD MAKE A LOVELIER QUEEN THAN THAT SKINNY REDHEAD."
CHARLES LOOKS DOWN AT THE FRECKLED FACE AND GRINS: "IT SEEMS I HAVE BEEN WAITING ALL MY LIFE FOR A SKINNY REDHEAD. WILL YOU MARRY ME..... BY THE WAY, WHAT IS YOUR NAME?"

THE TWINS ARE IN DARK DESPAIR. SUFFERING FROM AN ACUTE CASE OF PUPPY LOVE FOR YOUNG CUDDOCK OF WALES, THEY HAVE COPIED THE TRICKS AND SCHEMES USED BY THEIR ELDERS TO NO AVAIL.
"GROWNUPS KNOW NOTHING OF ROMANCE," ANNOUNCES VALETA. "I WONDER HOW MOTHER EVER WON OUR SIRE!"
"SORCERY," ANSWERS KAREN, "OR MAYBE A LOVE POTION."

IF GRACE AND AILIANORA MOURN THE LOSS OF SIR CHARLES, THEY HIDE THEIR BROKEN HEARTS WELL.
"HEARTLESS WENCHES," SNEERS KAREN. "THEY SOON FORGET, WHILE OUR LOVE FOR CUDDOCK WILL LAST FOREVER."
"WE WILL ENTER A CONVENT AND EASE OUR SORROW BY DOING GOOD WORKS," ANNOUNCES VALETA.

THE DAY COMES WHEN KING CUDDOCK MUST LEAD HIS HORSEMEN BACK TO NORTH WALES. AND KAREN'S GIFT IS A DOLL'S HEAD OF WOOD, BEAUTIFULLY CARVED. VALETA'S IS A KERCHIEF: "I EMBROIDERED IT MYSELF."
"WHY DO YOU GIVE ME YOUR MOST PRECIOUS POSSESSIONS?" HE ASKS.
"BECAUSE WE LOVE YOU," IS KAREN'S POSITIVE STATEMENT.

1441   9-20

IT IS RECORDED THAT, WHEN KING CUDDOCK RETURNED TO CAMELOT YEARS LATER TO ENTER A TOURNAMENT, HE WORE A WOODEN DOLL'S HEAD ON HIS CREST, A LADY'S KERCHIEF ON THE SHOULDER OF HIS SWORD ARM.
NEXT WEEK— The Missing Scroll

Prince Valiant
IN THE DAYS OF KING ARTHUR
BY Harold R Foster

Our Story FALTERS, FOR ONE OF THE ANCIENT PARCHMENT SCROLLS UPON WHICH THE SAGA OF PRINCE VALIANT IS WRITTEN HAS CRUMBLED WITH AGE SO THAT THE SCHOLARS CANNOT TRANSLATE THE FINE LATIN TEXT.

BUT THE AUTHOR THINKS IT IS SAFE TO ASSUME THAT SIR CHARLES RODE WESTWARD INTO CORNWALL WITH HIS THIN, RED-HAIRED BRIDE, FIRMLY CONVINCED THAT BEAUTY IS MEASURED BY THE NUMBER OF FRECKLES.

IN THIS ROMANTIC AGE TROUBADORS SING OF BROKENHEARTED MAIDENS FLINGING THEMSELVES FROM CASTLE BATTLEMENTS, BUT WITH SO MANY HANDSOME YOUNG NOBLES AROUND WE BELIEVE GRACE AND AILIANORA DID QUITE OTHERWISE.

BECAUSE OF THEIR GREAT LOVE FOR YOUNG KING CUDDOCK, THE TWINS PLAN TO ENTER A CONVENT AND DEVOTE THEIR LIVES TO DOING GOOD WORKS. BUT WE DOUBT VERY MUCH IF THEY ALLOWED THEIR SORROW TO SPOIL THEIR APPETITES OR KEEP THEM FROM THEIR NORMAL ACTIVITIES.

WHATEVER ADVENTURES WERE RECORDED ON THE DAMAGED SCROLL WE WILL NEVER KNOW, BUT WHEN THE TALE IS RESUMED, PRINCE VALIANT AND HIS FAMILY ARE ON BOLTAR'S GREAT DRAGON-SHIP HEADING NORTH AND FAR FROM SHORE. FROM THIS WE CONCLUDE THAT VAL HAS BEEN SUMMONED BY HIS FATHER, KING AGUAR OF THULE, AND DANGER LURKS ALONG THE COAST.

MIDDAY, AND THE LENGTH OF THE SHADOW CAST BY THE SUN INDICATES THAT THEY HAVE REACHED A CERTAIN LATITUDE. BOLTAR ORDERS THE SHIP TURNED TO THE EAST AND HIS MEN TO LOOK TO THEIR WEAPONS.

NEXT WEEK—*Bergen*

9-27-64   1442

Prince Valiant
IN THE DAYS OF KING ARTHUR
BY HAROLD R. FOSTER

Our Story: BOLTAR SWINGS HIS DRAGONSHIP TOWARD THE MISTY COAST, AND HIS SEA ROVERS PLACE THEIR WEAPONS NEAR AT HAND AS THEY RUN OUT THE OARS.

THEY COME IN BETWEEN THE ISLANDS CAUTIOUSLY AND APPROACH THE LITTLE BOAT-BUILDING VILLAGE OF BERGEN. ANXIOUS EYES WATCH THEIR APPROACH AND ARMS ARE PLACED IN READINESS.

A MESSENGER GREETS THEM: "A HOSTILE FLEET IS MAKING ITS DESTRUCTIVE WAY UP THE COAST," HE ANNOUNCES, "AND SOMEWHERE INLAND AN ARMY MARCHES. SHOULD THE TWO UNITE AT TRONDHEIMFJORD ALL THULE WILL BE LOST."

BOLTAR AND THE ROYAL FAMILY HEAD FOR THE SAFETY OF THE OPEN SEA WHILE PRINCE VALIANT AND THE GUIDE SAIL THE INSHORE ROUTE TO THE MIGHTY SOGNEFJORD. NOW HIS GUIDE TELLS VAL OF THE DANGER THAT BESETS THULE.

"SKOGUL ODERSON HAS RECRUITED A WILD AND LAWLESS CREW FROM AMONG THE BALTIC TRIBES, LANDED THEM IN OSLOFJORD AND EVEN NOW IS MARCHING UP THE VALLEY TOWARD KING AGUAR'S STRONGHOLD."

"AT EVERY HOMESTEAD AND FARM HE GIVES HIS CAPTIVES THEIR CHOICE; SWEAR THE OATH OF LOYALTY..... OR DIE. THAT THE RUTHLESS AND CRUEL SKOGUL IS ALSO HALF MAD MAKES NO DIFFERENCE TO HIS BAND."

AT THE HEAD OF THE FJORD THEY LEAVE THE BOAT AND FOLLOW THE FJELL INLAND. THE COLD BREATH OF THE GLACIER COMES DOWN TO THEM, AND WHEN THE TATTERED RAIN CLOUDS PART, THE BLUE ICE FIELD CAN BE SEEN, AND MELTING WATER STREAKS THE MOUNTAINSIDE WITH FOAMING STREAMS.

NEXT WEEK— **Garm the Hunter**

1443   10-4

Prince Valiant
IN THE DAYS OF KING ARTHUR
BY HAROLD R FOSTER

Our Story: PRINCE VALIANT AND HIS COMPANION HAVE PASSED THROUGH THE COASTAL MOUNTAINS. THE GROUND NOW SLOPES AWAY. "WE ARE TO MEET A SCOUT HEREABOUTS WHO HAS INFORMATION ON THE INVASION," SAYS NALL.

VAL LOOKS AT THE VAST EXPANSE OF FORESTED HILLS WITH THEIR RIVERS, VALLEYS AND LAKES. "SKOGUL COULD HIDE HIS WHOLE WAR BAND IN THIS WILDERNESS," SAYS VAL. "HOW CAN ONE SCOUT FIND US TWO?"
"THIS IS A VERY SPECIAL SCOUT," SMILES NALL.

THEY REACH A LAKE WHERE A MAN WAITS BESIDE A BOAT, AND THE MAN LOOKS FAMILIAR. "GARM!" SHOUTS VAL, "HOW GLAD I AM TO SEE YOU AGAIN. NALL, THIS IS GARM, HUNTSMAN TO MY FATHER, THE KING, AND TEACHER OF WOODCRAFT TO MY SON, ARN."

"THIS SKOGUL ODERSON IS EITHER A GENIUS OR A MADMAN," REPORTS GARM. "HIS FLEET IS IN THE SOUTH, THREATENING RAIDS TO THE NORTHWARD. YOUR SIRE'S HARDY VIKINGS MUST BE KEPT IN READINESS TO MEET THAT THREAT. MEANWHILE SKOGUL MARCHES QUIETLY NORTHWARD. BROKEN UP INTO SMALL BANDS, HIS ARMY IS ALMOST INVISIBLE IN THIS VAST FOREST!"

FOR MANY DAYS THE THREE SCOUTS MAKE THEIR WAY SOUTHWARD, HOPING TO MAKE CONTACT WITH THE INVADING FORCES TO DETERMINE THEIR COURSE AND THEIR STRENGTH.

AT LAST THEY MEET REFUGEES FLEEING NORTHWARD IN PANIC AND TELLING TALES OF SAVAGERY THAT ARE SHOCKING EVEN IN THESE ROUGH TIMES.

1444

10-11

HAL FOSTER

SOMEWHERE OUT THERE AMID THE LAKES AND RIVERS AND FOREST-COVERED HILLS THE ENEMY IS ADVANCING LIKE A PLAGUE OF LOCUSTS, DEVOURING THE COUNTRY AS THEY GO.
NEXT WEEK— **The Equalizer**

Prince Valiant
IN THE DAYS OF KING ARTHUR
BY Harold R Foster

Our Story: PRINCE VALIANT TRIES TO RAISE AN ARMY TO RESIST THE FORCES OF SKOGUL, BUT ALWAYS IT IS THE SAME ANSWER: "WHY SHOULD I LEAVE ALL I HAVE TO FIGHT FOR KING AGUAR? NO! I AM OLE OLESON AND I STAY HERE AND FIGHT FOR WHAT IS MINE!"

"BOATS ARE COMING UP THE LAKE," SAYS GARM, "POSSIBLY REFUGEES WHO HAVE ESCAPED THE ENEMY."
"THEN THEY WILL HAVE LOST EVERYTHING," VAL PONDERS. "WITH NOTHING TO LOSE AND MUCH TO GAIN THEY MIGHT BE THE BEGINNINGS OF A RESISTANCE FORCE."

THE REFUGEES TELL OF A NIGHT RAID WHEN SCREAMING SAVAGES STORMED THE PALISADES AND BROUGHT FIRE AND DEATH. IN ANSWER TO VAL'S QUESTION, THE MEN SAY: "YES, WE WILL JOIN YOUR BAND. WE WILL DO ANYTHING TO AVENGE THE SLAUGHTER OF OUR FRIENDS."

VAL LEADS THE WAY BACK TO OLE OLESON'S STEAD. THE PALISADE IS STRONG AND THE HOUSE SERFS AND SHEPHERDS NUMBER ABOUT TWENTY STOUT MEN. BUT THE EXPECTED RAIDERS MUSTER OVER ONE HUNDRED. VAL LOOKS FOR AN EQUALIZER.

THE STREAM THAT WATERS THE FARM LOOKS PROMISING. IT WIDENS INTO A POND FILLED WITH LOGS OLE HAS CUT FOR A NEW BUILDING AND, BEST OF ALL, THE STREAM ENTERS THROUGH A NARROW CHANNEL.

10-18

HAL FOSTER

ALL HANDS ARE PUT TO WORK ON A DAM THAT WILL HOLD BACK THE WATER. BY THE LIGHT OF FIRES THEY WORK THROUGH THE NIGHT, FOR VAL IS PLANNING A BATH FOR THE RAIDERS.

NEXT WEEK— Scouts

1445

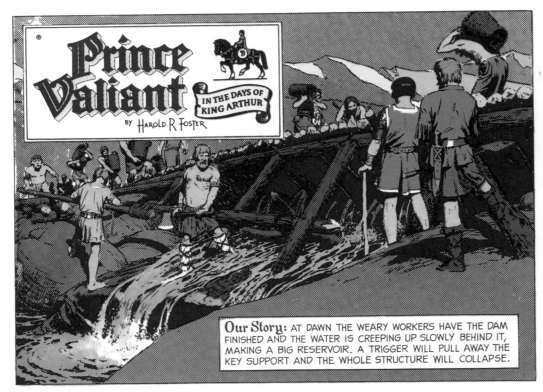

Our Story: AT DAWN THE WEARY WORKERS HAVE THE DAM FINISHED AND THE WATER IS CREEPING UP SLOWLY BEHIND IT, MAKING A BIG RESERVOIR. A TRIGGER WILL PULL AWAY THE KEY SUPPORT AND THE WHOLE STRUCTURE WILL COLLAPSE.

"NOW IT IS TIME TO SEND OUT SCOUTS TO FIND OUT WHERE OUR ENEMIES ARE," SAYS VAL.
"IT IS NOT NECESSARY," ANSWERS GARM, "FOR I HAVE A THOUSAND SCOUTS AT WORK. LISTEN."

"IN THE DISTANCE YOU HEAR A CROW CALL. WERE IT A FIGHTING CALL OR A FOOD CALL OTHER CROWS WOULD ANSWER, BUT THAT WAS A DANGER CALL, A WARNING. SEE THE DOE AND HER FAWN? SHE IS ALERT BUT MOVING SLOWLY AWAY FROM A SOURCE OF DANGER. THERE ARE MORE SMALL BIRDS ABOUT THAN USUAL. THEY HAVE BEEN DISTURBED AT THEIR FEEDING."

TWO HOURS PASS, THEN A SENTINEL CROW SILENTLY TAKES ITS PERCH ON A TALL TREE. A FINE BUCK, ANTLERS BACK AND TAIL WAVING GOES LEAPING BY AND THE MAGPIES SET UP A CLAMOR.
"IT IS TIME TO GO. OUR ENEMIES WILL BE HERE SHORTLY."

OLE RECEIVES THEIR WARNING WITH HEAVY SARCASM. "SO, YOU NEVER EVEN SAW THE RAIDERS, BUT YOU TELL ME THEY WILL BE HERE WITHIN THE HOUR. ARE YOU CHILDREN THAT YOU BELIEVE WHAT THE LITTLE BIRDIES AND BUTTERFLIES TELL YOU?"

"DON'T YOU WISH YOU HAD THE BRAINS OF A BUTTERFLY, OLE?" AND GARM POINTS ACROSS THE CLEARING WHERE THE RAIDERS ALREADY ARE GATHERING. OLE SLAMS AND BARS THE GATES. "OH, WOTAN," HE PRAYS, "MAKE ME AS WISE AS A BUTTERFLY!"

NEXT WEEK— **Bath Night**

10-25   1446

Prince Valiant
IN THE DAYS OF KING ARTHUR
BY Harold R. Foster

WITH WILD YELLS THE ATTACK BEGINS, AND VAL SIGNALS THE TRUMPETER. SPEARS AND THROWING AXES FILL THE AIR AS THE MOB POURS INTO THE DRY RIVER BED IN FRONT OF THE DEFENSES.

Our Story: FROM BEHIND THE STOUT PALISADE THAT GUARDS OLESON'S FARM PRINCE VALIANT WATCHES THE ENEMY PREPARE FOR THE ATTACK. TREES ARE FELLED AND STEPS NOTCHED IN THEM FOR SCALING THE WALLS. A HUGE LOG WILL SERVE AS A RAM.

FAR UP THE STREAM THEY HEAR THE TRUMPET'S CALL. THE DAM IS OPENED AND WITH A ROAR THE PENT-UP WATER FOAMS DOWN THE DRY BED.

IT IS NOT THAT THE RAIDERS OBJECT TO AN OCCASIONAL BATH, BUT THIS IS OVERDOING IT. IT IS DOUBTFUL IF ANY ONE OF THEM EVER WILL TAKE ANOTHER!

FOR A WHILE IT LOOKS AS IF VAL HAS CARRIED OUT HIS PLAN TOO WELL AND THE FARM BUILDINGS WILL BE WASHED AWAY, TOO, BUT THE PALISADE BREAKS THE FORCE OF THE FLOOD.

THE LOOT LEFT BEHIND BY THE RAIDERS IS CONSIDERABLE. THE GREAT AMOUNT OF WEAPONS GIVES VAL AN IDEA. IT IS SO DESPERATE, SO DANGEROUS THAT ITS VERY AUDACITY MAY BRING SUCCESS.

NEXT WEEK - The Gadfly

1447   11-1

Our Story: PRINCE VALIANT OPENED A DAM AND WASHED OUT A RAID. LEFT BEHIND IS THE LOOT OF MONTHS OF RAIDING AND ENOUGH WEAPONS FOR A HUNDRED MEN. WHEN THE SPOILS ARE DIVIDED OLE OLESON WILL BE WEALTHY FOR LIFE. VAL SETS OUT TO FIND HIMSELF AN ARMY.

SKOGUL ODERSON LEADS HIS FIERCE HOST NORTHWARD TOWARD VIKINGSHOLM, KING AGUAR'S STRONGHOLD, AND HE HAS ORDERED THAT NOTHING LIVING SHOULD SURVIVE THEIR PASSING.

AND THE ARMY IS BROKEN UP INTO GROUPS OF A HUNDRED OR MORE, FOR THIS IS A COUNTRY OF FARMS AND SMALL VILLAGES, AND SWORD AND FLAME COME TO THEM BEFORE THEY KNOW AN ENEMY IS NEAR.

KING AGUAR CALLS IN HIS CHIEFTAINS AND PREPARES FOR WAR. BUT WHERE? IT IS KNOWN THAT SKOGUL LANDED AN ARMY AT OSLOFJORD AND THEN VANISHED AMID THE HILLS AND FORESTS. EVEN THE KING'S SCOUTS CANNOT ESTIMATE THE NUMBER OR THE DIRECTION OF THE SCATTERED BANDS.

AND NEITHER DOES VAL. HE IS CONTENT TO SEEK THEM OUT ONE AT A TIME AND DESTROY THEM SOMEHOW. AND HE WILL NOT HAVE FAR TO SEEK, FOR A GROUP OF BOATS CAN BE SEEN IN THE DISTANCE, AND VAL, WHO HAS AS YET ONLY TWENTY MEN, SEEKS A DEFENSIVE POSITION.

"WHY IS THIS GREAT PILE OF LOGS HERE, GARM?" HE ASKS.
"THEY WILL BE ROLLED INTO THE STREAM WHEN THE WATER IS HIGH ENOUGH AND TAKEN TO THE VILLAGE WHERE, THIS WINTER, THEY WILL BE HEWN INTO BUILDING TIMBERS."

ACROSS THE RIVER A TREE IS FELLED, BLOCKING THE CHANNEL ON THAT SIDE.

THE WATER IS SWIFT HERE AND THE RAIDERS MUST HAUL THEIR BOATS UP. "I AM GREATLY TEMPTED TO TUMBLE THESE LOGS DOWN, GARM." "I WILL HELP YOU, MY PRINCE," ANSWERS GARM, TAKING UP HIS AXE.
NEXT WEEK—The Gadfly Stings Again

Prince Valiant
IN THE DAYS OF KING ARTHUR
BY Harold R Foster

Our Story: A BAND OF THE RAIDERS THAT ARE LAYING WASTE THE LAND OF THULE HAS CROSSED THE LAKE AND REACHED THE SWIFT WATER BELOW PRINCE VALIANT'S POSITION. THEY LOOK UP AS VAL SHOUTS TO HIS SCANTY FOLLOWERS TO TAKE THEIR POSITIONS.

THEN HE AND GARM DRIVE HOME THE WEDGES THAT WILL RELEASE THE STACKED LOGS.

AN AVALANCHE OF TIMBER ROARS DOWN THE SLOPE, DROWNING OUT THE SCREAMS OF TERROR FROM THE WAR BAND AS, HELPLESS, THEY AWAIT THEIR FATE.

MOST OF THE BOATS ARE CRUSHED UNDER THE LOGS, OTHERS CAPSIZED BY THE HUGE WAVE THEY CREATE. THOSE WHO SURVIVE FIND VAL'S ARCHERS AND SPEARMEN LINING THE SHORE. AND THEY ARE SMILING!

NO ATTENTION IS PAID TO THOSE WHO ESCAPE BY SWIMMING TO THE OPPOSITE SHORE. THEY ARE UNARMED, FOR HAD THEY RETAINED ARMS OR ARMOR OF ANY KIND, THEY WOULD HAVE DROWNED.

RUMORS SPREAD, EVEN IN THIS SPARSELY SETTLED LAND. TALES OF SKOGUL'S BANDITS, THEIR MYSTERIOUS APPEARANCES AND HORRIBLE DEEDS HAVE FILLED THE SETTLERS WITH FEAR. VAL FINDS MANY RECRUITS, BUT HE CHOOSES AND ARMS ONLY THE BEST.

"TILL NOW WE HAVE BEEN AHEAD OF SKOGUL'S WAR BANDS AND COULD CHOOSE OUR OWN POSITION. NOW ONE BAND IS AHEAD OF US, FOR SEE, MY PRINCE, SOME LANDOWNERS' BUILDINGS HAVE BEEN PUT TO THE TORCH!"
NEXT WEEK-Val Joins the Enemy

1449

11-15

Our Story: PRINCE VALIANT AND HIS BAND FIND THE SOURCE OF THE SMOKE AND FLAME THEY SAW THE EVENING BEFORE. THE FIERCE RUFFIANS OF SKOGUL'S INVADING ARMY HAVE BROUGHT FIRE AND DEATH TO A LARGE FARMSTEAD, AND VAL ALLOWS HIS HARDY TROOP PLENTY OF TIME TO VIEW THE HORRORS. LUCKY THE ONES WHO DIED FIGHTING; THE REST MUST HAVE WELCOMED DEATH AT THE LAST.

"THESE WERE YOUR OWN PEOPLE," SAYS VAL. "NEVER FORGET WHAT YOU SEE BEFORE YOU. WHEN WE FIND THE FIENDS WHO DID THIS DEED THESE VICTIMS MUST BE AVENGED!"

GARM PICKS UP THE TRAIL. "I SEE NO TRACKS OF HORSES, AND THE DEPTH OF THEIR FOOTPRINTS SHOWS THEY ARE WEIGHED DOWN WITH PLUNDER. WE SHOULD OVERTAKE THEM BY NIGHTFALL. THEY NUMBER OVER A HUNDRED."

BUT IT IS ONLY A FEW HOURS LATER THAT THEY WALK RIGHT INTO THE ENEMY. GARM, WHO IS LEADING, SIGNALS TO THOSE BEHIND HIM AND JOINS HIS FOES IN CUTTING TREES AND NOTCHING THEM TO MAKE SCALING LADDERS. NO ONE PAYS ANY ATTENTION TO THE NEW ADDITION TO SKOGUL'S FORCES.

VAL CHANGES TO LESS CONSPICUOUS COSTUME AND SCOUTS THE TARGET OF THE ATTACK, A COLLECTION OF HOUSES, BARNS AND CATTLE BYRES SURROUNDED BY A STRONG PALISADE. ALREADY THE HOUSE CARLS MAN THE WALLS, AND SERFS AND BONDSMEN ARE RUNNING IN FROM THE FIELDS.

1450

11-22

NOW THE RAIDERS LEAVE THE WOODS AND FORM IN LINE AT THE EDGE OF THE CLEARING, AND IN THE LAST ROW IS PRINCE VALIANT AND HIS BAND. THEN THE WAR DRUMS THUNDER AND THE SCREAMING HORDE RACES ACROSS THE OPEN GROUND.

NEXT WEEK– The Mysterious Rearguard

Prince Valiant
IN THE DAYS OF KING ARTHUR
BY HAROLD R FOSTER

Our Story: THE DOUGHTY CHIEFTAIN BELLOWS DEFIANCE AT THE APPROACHING RAIDERS, AND HIS YOUNG HOUSE CARLS MAKE READY TO DEFEND THE PALISADE. THEN A STRANGE THING IS NOTICED. THE ADVANCING HORDE IS LEAVING A TRAIL OF VERY DEAD RUFFIANS BEHIND!

IN THE DIM FOREST PRINCE VALIANT'S MEN HAVE MINGLED WITH THE RAIDERS UNNOTICED, BUT WHEN THE ORDER IS GIVEN TO CHARGE ACROSS THE OPEN, VAL AND HIS BAND ARE IN THE LAST RANK. SILENTLY, EFFICIENTLY THEY SET ABOUT EVENING THE ODDS.

THE CHARGE HAS ALMOST REACHED THE PALISADE BEFORE THE TRICK IS DISCOVERED AND THE RAIDERS TURN ON VAL'S WAR BAND THEN THE DEFENDERS HEAR A WELCOME CRY: "AGUAR! THULE! THULE! THULE!"

THE GATES SWING WIDE AND THE DEFENDERS SWARM OUT ECHOING THE WAR CRY. FOR A WHILE THE RAIDERS STAND FIRM, BUT FINDING THEMSELVES ATTACKED FROM BOTH FRONT AND REAR THEY FEEL A GROWING SENSE OF PANIC.

NO PRISONERS ARE TAKEN, FEW ESCAPE. FOR VAL'S MEN HAVE SEEN A SAMPLE OF THEIR SENSELESS BRUTALITY, AND THE LUST FOR REVENGE IS UPON THEM. BY SUNDOWN THE DEED IS DONE. THE SPOILS AND THE WOUNDED ARE BROUGHT INTO THE VILLAGE, AND THE BURIAL PARTY BEGINS ITS GRIM WORK.

1451

11-29-64

IT IS TIME FOR SKOGUL ODERSON TO CALL HIS WAR BANDS TOGETHER FOR THE FINAL MARCH ON VIKINGSHOLM, BUT THREE OF THESE BANDS HAVE DISAPPEARED.

NEXT WEEK—**The Mysterious Monster**

Our Story: "WE HAVE MET AND DESTROYED THREE OF SKOGUL'S WAR BANDS. HE MUST HAVE LEARNED OF THIS BY NOW AND WILL MOST LIKELY SEND BACK A STRONG FORCE TO FIND THE CAUSE. GARM, SCOUT HIS POSITION AND LEARN WHAT YOU CAN."

SKOGUL HAS REACHED THE PLACE WHERE HIS WILD FOLLOWERS WERE TO RENDEZVOUS, BUT THERE IS NO TRACE OF HIS THREE MOST DESTRUCTIVE WAR BANDS.

GARM FOLLOWS SKOGUL'S TRAIL, WHICH LEADS UP THE RIVER VALLEY, THEN VEERS SHARPLY NORTHEAST INTO THE HILLS. THIS IS THE ROUTE BY WHICH SKOGUL COULD COME DOWN SUDDENLY UPON TRONDHEIM AND AN OPEN ROAD TO THE STRONGHOLD AT VIKINGSHOLM.

HE RETURNS SWIFTLY AND REPORTS TO PRINCE VALIANT: "SKOGUL HAS COMMITTED HIS ARMY TO ITS INTENDED ROUTE, AND WE CAN NOW SEND POSITIVE INFORMATION TO THE KING. HE IS ALSO SENDING A STRONG FORCE TO FIND OUT WHAT HAPPENED TO HIS MISSING WARRIORS."

THE FATE OF THE LOST WAR BANDS IS ALL TOO CLEAR. A FEARFUL MONSTER HAD COME OUT OF THE SOMBER FORESTS AND DEVOURED THEM. SOME OF THE CRUSHED AND TORN GEAR IS RECOGNIZED. IT IS A FRIGHTENING TALE SKOGUL'S MEN WILL TAKE BACK!

"GARM, YOU ARE TO STAY IN THE REAR AND REPORT ANY CHANGE IN THE ENEMY PLANS. NALL AND I WILL TAKE TWENTY MEN, CIRCLE THE ENEMY, AND HEAD FOR VIKINGSHOLM."

IT IS ROUGH TRAVELING THROUGH FORESTS AND OVER HILLS, BUT AT LAST THEY CIRCLE SKOGUL'S FORCES.

"NOW I MUST TRAVEL ALONE AND FAST. NALL, YOU AND YOUR MEN ARE TO LEAVE MONSTER FOOTPRINTS WHEREVER THEY WILL DO THE MOST GOOD.

NEXT WEEK— **The Figurehead**

1452 © King Features Syndicate, Inc., 1964. World rights reserved. 12-6-64

Prince Valiant
IN THE DAYS OF KING ARTHUR
BY HAROLD R. FOSTER

Our Story: PRINCE VALIANT BEGINS HIS LONG JOURNEY TO VIKINGSHOLM TO WARN THE KING OF THE APPROACH OF THE INVADING ARMY, AND NALL IS LEFT TO SPREAD FEAR IN THE APPROACHING HOST.

AND NALL HAS A GRIM SENSE OF HUMOR. A BEAR IS SLAIN, AND AFTER THEY TAKE WHAT MEAT THEY NEED, THE REST IS TORN INTO SHREDS, EVEN THE BONES CRUSHED AS IF THE MONSTER STOPPED FOR A LIGHT LUNCH.

AT A RIVER CROSSING NALL CREATES HIS MASTERPIECE. FOR THERE IN THE SOFT EARTH OF THE BANK IS EVIDENCE THAT THE MONSTER HAS LEAPED SEVENTY FEET!
SKOGUL HAD SCOURED THE BALTIC PORTS FOR RECRUITS, CHOOSING ONLY THE MOST BRUTAL......

.....WHO, LIKE MOST OF THEIR KIND, ARE SUPERSTITIOUS AND FEAR THE UNKNOWN. THEY ARE USED TO THE DANGERS OF THE SEA, BUT THESE SOMBER FORESTS WHERE MONSTERS DWELL FILL THEM WITH TERROR. THEY ARE CLOSE TO MUTINY, BUT SKOGUL DRAWS HIS SWORD AND CUTS DOWN THE RINGLEADERS.

NALL LEADS HIS SMALL BAND INTO TRONDHEIM TO WARN THE PEOPLE OF THE APPROACHING DANGER. IN THE SHIPYARDS HE SEES A DRAGON FIGUREHEAD BEING PREPARED FOR ONE OF THE LONGSHIPS. IT IS SO DELIGHTFULLY HIDEOUS THAT HE BORROWS IT.

1453

12-13-64

BESIDE THE TRAIL BY WHICH THE ENEMY MUST APPROACH THE TOWN HE SETS UP HIS 'MONSTER'.

NEXT WEEK — **The Berserker**

Prince Valiant
IN THE DAYS OF KING ARTHUR
BY HAROLD R FOSTER

Our Story: NALL SETS UP THE FIGUREHEAD BESIDE THE TRAIL BY WHICH THE RAIDERS MUST COME, AND THEN SETTLES DOWN TO WAIT.

SKOGUL'S CONQUERING HORDE IS NOW BUT A FEAR-STRICKEN MOB AND AT SIGHT OF THE DRAGON GUARDING THE TRAIL, THEY HALT.

BUT WHEN THE DRAGON SLOWLY TURNS ITS HEAD TOWARD THEM, AND A TERRIBLE ROAR ECHOES THROUGH THE HILLS, THEIR TERROR IS MORE THAN THEIR FEAR OF THE CHIEFTAIN.

SKOGUL DOES NOT RUN. HIS TWISTED MIND IS FILLED WITH GREATER HORRORS. THE SLAVES WHO CARRY HIS PERSONAL THINGS CANNOT FLEE WITH THE REST; THEY ARE CHAINED.

HE ORDERS THESE SLAVES TO PREPARE A DRAUGHT FROM THE MYSTERIOUS SACRED MUSHROOMS AND DRAINS THE CUP. THE DRUG TAKES EFFECT AND HIS MADNESS BECOMES COMPLETE.

SKOGUL ODERSON HAS BECOME A BERSERKER AND MUST KILL ALL LIVING THINGS UNTIL HE HIMSELF IS KILLED. WOE TO MAN OR BEAST THAT IS IN HIS PATH!

12-20 © King Features Syndicate, Inc. 1964. World rights reserved. 1454

A SMALL BOY, DIPPING FOR SALMON FROM A FLIMSY SCAFFOLD, SEES HIM COMING, THE DRIPPING SWORD EVIDENCE OF HIS INTENT.

THE RUSHING RIVER COVERS THE HEAVILY-ARMED LEADER OF A CONQUERING HORDE, DEFEATED AT LAST BY A BOY ARMED ONLY WITH A NET AND A WET FISH.

NEXT WEEK— **The War's End**

Our Story: PRINCE VALIANT TROTS WEARILY INTO VIKINGSHOLM TO BRING WARNING OF AN INVADING ARMY, NOT KNOWING THAT THE ARMY IS NOW FLEEING IN TERROR AND THAT THEIR LEADER HAS MET HIS DOOM BY WAY OF A DEAD FISH.

IN SPITE OF HIS FAMILY'S ENERGETIC WELCOME, VAL IS ABLE TO BRING HIS MESSAGE TO HIS FATHER, THE KING.

THEN FROM THE MOUNTAIN TOPS THE SIGNAL FIRES GIVE THEIR WARNING. A COLUMN OF SMOKE BY DAY, A BLAZE AT NIGHT, AND THE HARDY SEAFARERS MAN THEIR LONGSHIPS AND BEAT TIME TO THE WAR SONGS WITH THEIR OARS.

FIRST TO ARRIVE IS BOLTAR, THE SEA KING. WHEN HE HEARS THAT SKOGUL'S ARMY AND FLEET OF SHIPS ARE TO MEET AND ATTACK VIKINGSHOLM BY BOTH LAND AND SEA HE IS MOST GENEROUS: "YOU, SIRE, CAN HAVE THE ARMY. MY BOYS AND I WILL TAKE CARE OF THEIR NAVY."

AND WHEN THAT NAVY SAILS INTO THE FJORD IT IS NOT SKOGUL'S ARMY THAT AWAITS THEM, BUT THAT OF KING AGUAR, AND RIGHT BEHIND THEM COME BOLTAR AND HIS 'BOYS'. AS THIS BECAME SOMETHING IN THE NATURE OF LIGHT EXERCISE RATHER THAN A BATTLE, IT IS NOT FURTHER RECORDED.

1455

12-27-64

PRINCE ARN HAS TAKEN PART IN THE VICTORY ABOARD BOLTAR'S DRAGONSHIP, AND BOLTAR'S SON IS ALSO THERE. "HAVE YOU FORGOTTEN THE PROMISE YOUR MOTHER, THE SUN WOMAN, MADE TO MY PEOPLE?" HE ASKS.

NEXT WEEK— **The Oath**

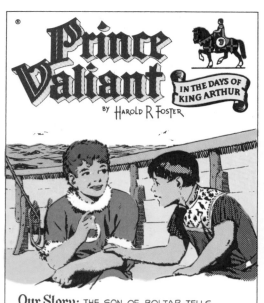

Prince Valiant
IN THE DAYS OF KING ARTHUR
BY HAROLD R FOSTER

Our Story: THE SON OF BOLTAR TELLS PRINCE ARN OF A PROMISE MADE LONG AGO TO A PEOPLE WHO LIVED BEYOND THE WIDE SEA. "MY PEOPLE BELIEVED YOUR MOTHER TO BE THE SUN GODDESS, AND SHE PROMISED THAT ONE DAY YOU WOULD RETURN TO THEM. WILL YOU?"

"I REMEMBER THE STORY AS MY MOTHER TOLD IT," ANSWERS ARN. "ULFRUN, THE SEA HAWK, CAST HIS EYES UPON MY MOTHER AND DESIRED HER ABOVE ALL THINGS. HE STOLE HER FROM THE CASTLE."

"IN HIS GREAT WARSHIP HE SAILED WESTWARD, TOWARD UNKNOWN SEAS, AND WHEN THE RED SAILS OF MY SIRE'S SHIP SHOWED ON THE HORIZON HE LAUGHED, FOR NO ONE DARED FOLLOW WHERE HE, THE SEA HAWK, LED."

"THROUGH MIST AND RAIN ICELAND WAS DISCOVERED, BUT BECAUSE OF MOTHER'S FAIR HAIR AND GRAY EYES IT SEEMED UNIMPORTANT. ONLY BY ROWING INTO A WIND COULD ULFRUN OUTDISTANCE THE SAILING SHIP. BUT SOON THE RED SAILS WOULD BE AGAIN IN SIGHT."

"NO LONGER WAS ULFRUN LEADING HIS ENEMY TO DEFEAT; HE WAS FLEEING! LOVE TURNED TO HATE. HE STRUCK HIS CAPTIVE DOWN AND DREW HIS SWORD. HER SEWING WAS SPILLED UPON THE DECK, BABY CLOTHES. THEN ULFRUN KNEW PRINCE VALIANT WOULD NEVER GIVE UP THE CHASE!"

"LAND! AND THE GREAT UNKNOWN SEA HAD BEEN CROSSED. UP A HUGE RIVER, NEVER FAR APART, THEY WENT UNTIL STOPPED AT LAST BY NIAGARA. THE CHASE ENDED IN A CLASH OF SWORDS."

"ULFRUN FLED, BUT MY SIRE FOUND HIM AT THE EDGE OF THE CHASM AND DREW THE 'SINGING SWORD'!"

1456   © King Features Syndicate, Inc., 1964. World rights reserved.   1-3-65

"MY PARENTS WERE UNITED. 'I FOUND THIS BEFORE I LEFT AND KNEW I MUST FOLLOW YOU TO THE VERY END'."

NEXT WEEK—Tillicum's Story

HAL FOSTER

Prince Valiant

IN THE DAYS OF KING ARTHUR

BY Harold R. Foster

Our Story: "AND THAT," CONCLUDES PRINCE ARN, "IS THE STORY AS MY MOTHER TOLD IT, OF HOW MY PARENTS CROSSED THE UNKNOWN SEA AND CAME TO THE STRANGE LAND WHERE YOUR MOTHER, TILLICUM, LIVED WITH HER PEOPLE."

HATHA, SON OF BOLTAR, TAKES UP THE TALE: "WHEN THE VIKING SHIP LANDED, OUR PEOPLE GAZED IN AWE. NEVER HAD THEY SEEN A WOMAN WITH HAIR LIKE SUNLIGHT ON RIPENING GRAIN, EYES GREY AS THE RAIN. THEY CALLED HER THE SUN-WOMAN AND WORSHIPPED HER AS 'BRINGER OF HARVESTS'!"

"WHEN IT BECAME KNOWN THAT THE SUN-WOMAN WAS ABOUT TO BEAR A CHILD, THE CHIEFS ASSEMBLED AND BROUGHT MANY GIFTS, ONE OF WHICH WAS TILLICUM, MY MOTHER, AND SHE WAS BOUND TO SERVE THE 'BRINGER OF HARVESTS' FOREVERMORE."

"THE HARVEST WAS GOOD THAT AUTUMN, AND DURING THE WINTER GAME WAS PLENTIFUL, SO THAT THERE WAS NO FAMINE WHEN SPRING CAME. AND THAT SPRING YOU, ARN, WERE BORN AND THE STALWART VIKINGS WHO SERVED YOUR MOTHER HAILED YOU AS A FUTURE CHIEFTAIN."

1457

"WHEN THE SHIP WAS MADE READY FOR THE PERILOUS JOURNEY BACK ACROSS THE GREAT SEA OUR PEOPLE CRIED; 'IF THE SUN-WOMAN LEAVES, WHO WILL BRING FERTILITY TO OUR PLANTING, RIPENESS TO OUR GRAIN?'"

"IT IS NOT BY ANY GIFT FROM ME THAT YOU WILL PROSPER BUT BY YOUR OWN WISDOM AND INDUSTRY. AND WHO KNOWS, SOME DAY MY SON MAY RETURN AND LEAD YOU TO GREATNESS!'"

"THEN I AM HONOR BOUND TO RETURN ACROSS THE SEA AND FULFILL MY MOTHER'S PROMISE," CRIES ARN, "AND YOU MUST COME WITH ME, HATHA!"

NEXT WEEK—The Oath Remembered

1-10-64

Prince Valiant
IN THE DAYS OF KING ARTHUR
BY HAROLD R FOSTER

Our Story: PRINCE ARN IS FIRED BY A GREAT AMBITION TO CROSS THE WILD SEA TO THE PLACE OF HIS BIRTH BESIDE THE GREAT FALLS THE NATIVES CALL NIAGARA.

BUT IT WILL BE SOME TIME BEFORE HE CAN DISCUSS HIS PLANS, FOR A FEAST IS BEING HELD TO CELEBRATE THE VICTORY OVER SKOGUL ODERSON AND HIS RUFFIAN ARMY, AND VIKINGSHOLM ROCKS WITH THE NOISE.

FROM A SMALL BALCONY THE ROYAL FAMILY SURVEYS THE WRECKAGE OF THE DINING HALL. *"VICTORY HAS ITS PRICE,"* SAYS THE KING RUEFULLY. *"OUR COFFERS HAVE BEEN EMPTIED FOR FOOD AND DRINK AND VIKINGSHOLM DEVASTATED IN THE INTERESTS OF HOSPITALITY."*

AT LAST ARN IS ABLE TO TELL HIS PARENTS OF HIS GREAT DESIRE TO VISIT THE LAND BEYOND THE SEA AND FULFILL HIS MOTHER'S PROMISE. HATHA TOO BEGS HIS PARENTS, BOLTAR AND TILLICUM, TO LET HIM SEE THE LAND FROM WHICH HIS MOTHER CAME.

"I DID NOT TELL YOU OF THE PROMISE I MADE," ANSWERS ALETA ANXIOUSLY, *"FOR YOU ARE SO YOUNG. I INTENDED TO WAIT UNTIL YOU WERE MORE MATURE, BUT NOW THAT YOU KNOW YOU WILL NOT BE CONTENT TILL MY PROMISE IS FULFILLED."*

1458   © King Features Syndicate, Inc., 1965. World rights reserved.   1-17

"SUMMER IS ENDING, YOU CANNOT START UNTIL SPRING. SO SPEND THE WINTER WITH US, LEARN TO SPEAK OUR TONGUE AND THE WAYS OF OUR PEOPLE."

AS THEY ROUND THE HEADLAND ON THEIR WAY TO BOLTAR'S STEAD ARN GAZES ACROSS THE WILD, GRAY, ENDLESS OCEAN. HE HAS A MOMENT OF MISGIVING. *"HAVE I THE WISDOM AND THE COURAGE TO CARRY ME THROUGH THIS QUEST?"*

NEXT WEEK— Boltarstead

Our Story: TO FULFILL A PROMISE MADE BY HIS MOTHER, PRINCE ARN ASKS PERMISSION TO VOYAGE ACROSS THE WIDE SEAS TO THE PLACE WHERE HE WAS BORN, A PLACE THE NATIVES CALL 'NIAGARA'. NOW THAT HIS PARENTS HAVE GIVEN THEIR PERMISSION HE IS BESET WITH DOUBTS: IS HE ABLE TO COMMAND, HAS HE THE WISDOM, THE EXPERIENCE, WILL HE FALTER DURING THE PERILOUS JOURNEY?

ARN HAS LITTLE TIME LEFT TO WORRY. WHEN BOLTAR LANDS HIS DRAGONSHIP BENEATH HIS FORTRESS-LIKE FARMSTEAD ARN FINDS EVERY WAKING HOUR FILLED WITH RESPONSIBILITIES.

GUNDAR HARL'S SAILING SHIP THAT MADE THE JOURNEY FOURTEEN YEARS AGO IS MADE READY. PROVISIONS, TOOLS, TRADE GOODS, WEAPONS AND ALL THE NECESSARY ITEMS FOR THE ADVENTURE MUST BE GATHERED BEFORE SPRING.

AUTUMN HAS BEEN A TIME FOR HAWKING OR RIDING OUT WITH HIS HOUNDS, BUT NOT NOW. NOW ARN MUST LEARN A STRANGE LANGUAGE AND STRANGER CUSTOMS.

SEAFARERS HAVE NEITHER COMPASS NOR SEXTANT TO AID THEIR NAVIGATION. THE NORTH STAR IS THEIR GUIDE AT NIGHT, BY DAY THE DIRECTION OF THE SUN'S SHADOW AT NOON, THE LENGTH OF THE SHADOW INDICATING THE LATITUDE.

BOLTAR'S SHIPS ARE DRAWN UP AND PRE-PARED FOR WINTER. GEAR IS REPAIRED AND STORED, AND THE VIKINGS, THE YEAR'S ROVING AT AN END, LEAVE FOR THEIR HOMES.

ARN TRIES TO RECRUIT SOME OF THEM FOR HIS GREAT ADVENTURE, BUT THEY ARE TOO ANXIOUS TO BE HOME WITH THEIR FAMILIES TO GIVE HIM HEED.

1459   © King Features Syndicate, Inc., 1965. World rights reserved.   1-24

VALIANT WARRIORS WILL FOLLOW HIS FATHER, SEEK TO SERVE BOLTAR THE SEA-KING, BUT WHO WILL DARE PERIL FOR A BOY?

NEXT WEEK— Recruiting

1459

Our Story: THE FIRST FROST...AND THE WOODS ARE BRIGHT WITH AUTUMN COLORS. ARN GAZES WISTFULLY AT THE SLEEK LINES OF GUNDAR HARL'S SAILING SHIP AND WONDERS HOW MANY OF ITS CREW WILL CONSENT TO SAIL ON THE GREAT ADVENTURE PLANNED FOR THE SPRING.

GUNDAR OFFERS LITTLE COMFORT: "MY CREW HAVE BECOME RICH BY OUR TRADING VENTURES, THEY MAY NOT CARE TO SAIL THE UNKNOWN SEA WITHOUT THE ASSURANCE OF GOOD PROFITS."

"I DOUBT IF ANY OF MY WARRIORS WILL VOLUNTEER FOR THE VOYAGE," BOLTAR ROARS IN HIS NORMAL VOICE, "YOU MAY ASK THEM, BUT THEY ARE USED TO ROVING, FIGHTING AND PLUNDER."

THEN TILLICUM RISES: "I, TILLICUM, WIFE OF BOLTAR, MOTHER OF HATHA, SAIL WITH GUNDAR IN THE SPRING TO MY HOMELAND, TO PRINCE ARN'S BIRTHPLACE. WE DO NOT WANT MEN OF VIOLENCE SEEKING PLUNDER, BUT THOSE WHO WILL TRADE IN FAIRNESS FOR RICH FURS, ORNAMENTS OF GOLD AND COPPER."

"LOOK, HATHA, YOUR MOTHER'S WORDS ARE HAVING EFFECT, NOT AMONG THE OLDER MEN WHO STICK TO OLD WAYS, BUT TO THE ADVENTUROUS YOUTHS!"

THE YOUNG MEN WILL HAVE SOMETHING TO TALK ABOUT DURING THE LONG WINTER MONTHS, BUT WILL THEIR ENTHUSIASM INCREASE OR WILL THEY SOON FORGET?

THE RESTLESS SEA GIVES WARNING OF WINTER GALES TO COME, BUT PRINCE ARN HAS AN IDEA AND SETS SAIL IN A FRAIL BOAT FOR VIKINGSHOLM.

NEXT WEEK—The Petition

Prince Valiant

IN THE DAYS OF KING ARTHUR

BY Harold R Foster

Our Story: THE AMBITIOUS VOYAGE PRINCE ARN HAS SET HIS HEART ON FACES FAILURE, FOR THE VIKING SEAFARERS ARE ONLY INTERESTED IN RAIDING AND PLUNDER. IN A SMALL SKIFF ARN SETS OUT FOR VIKINGSHOLM WITH A FAIR WIND.

WHEN HE TURNS INTO THE FJORD THE WIND IS AGAINST HIM, SO HE TAKES TO THE OARS. ALL THROUGH THE NIGHT HE ROWS. THE WIND GOES DOWN BUT THE BLISTERS GROW.

IT IS MID-MORNING WHEN HE REACHES VIKINGSHOLM. KING AGUAR IS HOLDING COURT, AND ARN REQUESTS THE CHAMBERLAIN TO ANNOUNCE HIM.

THE KING IS SURPRISED THAT HIS OWN GRANDSON APPEARS AS A PETITIONER. *"WHAT CAN WE DO FOR YOU, PRINCE ARN?"* *"IS IT NOT TRUE,"* ARN ASKS, *"THAT YEARS AGO YOU OFFERED A REWARD TO ANY OF YOUR SUBJECTS WHO DISCOVERED NEW LANDS AND OPENED NEW TRADE ROUTES?"*

"YES, SUCH IS THE LAW. THE TITLE OF EARL AND WIDE LANDS GO TO THE LEADER, AND EACH MEMBER OF THE CREW RECEIVES A FARM AND A FULL PURSE. BUT WHY DO YOU COME AS A PETITIONER WHEN YOU KNOW YOUR FAMILY WILL GIVE ALL THE HELP YOU NEED?"

"BECAUSE THIS IS MY ADVENTURE, SIRE," ARN REPLIES PROUDLY, *"AND I ASK NO FAVORS, ONLY WHAT IS RIGHTFULLY MINE."*

1461   © King Features Syndicate, Inc., 1965. World rights reserved.   2-7

ANOTHER OBSTACLE HAS BEEN CLEARED FROM THE HIGH ROAD TO ADVENTURE, BUT AT A PRICE: HE MUST LEAVE BEHIND ALL THE LOVE AND TENDERNESS HE HAS TAKEN FOR GRANTED THROUGH THE YEARS.

WITH THE DAWN ARN IS ON HIS WAY, AND THE WIND HOLDS FAIR FOR THE RUN DOWN THE TRONDHEIMFJORD.

NEXT WEEK—The Wreck

Our Story: THE WIND IS BRISK AND PRINCE ARN'S LITTLE CRAFT SAILS SWIFTLY ALONG IN THE SHELTER OF THE MANY ISLANDS. ONLY WHEN HE ROUNDS THE HEADLAND THAT GUARDS THE ENTRANCE OF THE FJORD WHERE BOLTAR LIVES IS HE FACED WITH THE FULL FORCE OF THE OPEN SEA.

AND HERE THE SAIL RIPS. FLAPPING WILDLY, IT THREATENS TO TEAR THE BOAT APART UNTIL ARN UNSHIPS THE USELESS MAST AND HEAVES IT OVERBOARD.

BY THE TIME HE GETS THE OARS OUT, WIND AND WAVE HAVE SWEPT THE LIGHT CRAFT PERILOUSLY CLOSE TO THE ROCKS.

INCH BY INCH HE IS LOSING GROUND. TO KEEP UP THE STRUGGLE ANY LONGER WILL LEAVE HIM TOO EXHAUSTED TO SAVE HIMSELF. DELIBERATELY HE RIDES THE NEXT BREAKER TOWARD THE MENACING ROCKS.

THE WAVE EXPLODES AGAINST THE ROCKS IN A WELTER OF FOAM, AND WHEN IT RECEDES THE SHATTERED SKIFF HANGS FOR A MOMENT ON A LEDGE.

ARN CLIMBS OUT OF REACH OF THE CLUTCHING BREAKERS AND LOOKS BACK. AS HE WATCHES THE POWER OF THE SEA TEAR HIS BOAT TO SPLINTERS, HE IS TREMBLING. HE HAS BEEN TOO BUSY TO FEEL FEAR UNTIL NOW.

HE FINDS A SHELTERED SPOT AND, WHILE HIS BODY IS STILL WARM FROM HIS EXERTIONS, WRINGS THE WATER FROM HIS CLOTHES.

NIGHT IS NEAR AND THERE IS A CHILL IN THE WIND THAT PROMISES FROST. HE SETS OUT TO FIND SHELTER, FIRE AND *FOOD.*

NEXT WEEK — *Recruits*

2-14-65   1462

Prince Valiant
IN THE DAYS OF KING ARTHUR
BY Harold R Foster

Our Story: PRINCE ARN HAS SURVIVED SHIPWRECK AND THE ANGER OF THE SEA, BUT IS DOUBTFUL IF HE CAN SURVIVE THE CHILL NIGHT WIND. ALREADY HIS DAMP CLOTHING IS STIFF WITH ICE.

HE LIFTS HIS HEAD AND TAKES A DEEP BREATH; YES, FAINT BUT UNMISTAKABLE, THE SMELL OF WOOD SMOKE.

FOLLOWING UPWIND HE CAN NOW SMELL CATTLE. THEN A DOG BARKS AND ARN SHOUTS A GREETING. A DOOR OPENS AND FLOODS THE DARKNESS WITH LIGHT.

IT IS UNSAFE TO APPROACH A VIKING HOUSE AT NIGHT, SO ARN STANDS OUTSIDE AND GIVES HIS NAME AND HIS REASON FOR BEING THERE. HE IS BIDDEN TO ENTER BY A DOORWAY SO CONSTRUCTED THAT A VISITOR, FOR THE MOMENT, IS HELPLESS.

ARN TELLS THEM OF HIS ADVENTURE AND HOW HE SAVED HIMSELF, AND THE VIKINGS NOD THEIR HEADS KNOWINGLY; THIS LAD IS ONE OF THE 'LUCKY ONES'. WHATEVER HE UNDERTAKES WILL END FAVORABLY.

THEN HE TELLS OF THE GREAT ADVENTURE HE HAS PLANNED FOR THE SPRING. "WE SAIL THE WIDE SEA WESTWARD UNTIL WE COME TO THE NEW LAND. THE KING WILL REWARD WITH A FARM AND A FULL PURSE ALL WHO RETURN."

IN THE MORNING A BOAT IS LAUNCHED AND ARN IS ROWED ACROSS THE FJORD TO BOLTAR'S STRONGHOLD. AND THE YOUNG CARLS ASK HIM MANY QUESTIONS ABOUT HIS PROPOSED VOYAGE AND THE REWARDS. ARN IS HOPEFUL. PERHAPS HE CAN GET A CREW AFTER ALL.

NEXT WEEK—The Salesman

14-63   2-21   HAL FOSTER

Our Story: PRINCE ARN RETURNS TO BOLTAR'S STRONGHOLD AND THE BOATMEN TELL OF HIS MIRACULOUS ESCAPE FROM THE HUNGRY SEA. THEY HAIL HIM AS ONE OF THE 'LUCKY ONES' WHOSE UNDERTAKINGS WILL PROSPER.

HE TELLS OF THE SUCCESS OF HIS MISSION; "KING AGUAR HAS REAFFIRMED HIS PROMISE OF A FARM AND A FULL PURSE TO ALL WHO DISCOVER NEW LANDS OR NEW TRADE ROUTES FOR THULE." THIS SOUNDS GOOD TO SOME OF THE YOUNG MEN FROM THE BOAT AND THEY ASK TO JOIN THE ADVENTURE PLANNED FOR THE SPRING

WHEN DARKNESS FALLS THE SKALD OFTTIMES TAKES HIS HARP AND SINGS A HERO-POEM, AND A GREAT FAVORITE WITH THE VIKINGS IS THE SAGA OF PRINCE VALIANT AND HOW HE SAILED TO THE WORLD'S EDGE TO RESCUE THE FAIR ALETA FROM ULFRUN, THE SEAHAWK.

"IT IS A TRULY GREAT POEM YOU HAVE COMPOSED, NOBLE SKALD, BUT IT LACKS A LAST VERSE: THE PROMISE THE LADY ALETA MADE THAT HER FIRST-BORN WOULD RETURN TO THAT FAR LAND. I, PRINCE ARN, AM THAT FIRST-BORN AND, WITH THE SPRING, I WILL RETURN TO FULFILL THAT VOW."

THE SKALD BECOMES A PUBLIC-RELATIONS MAN AND SETS FORTH ON THE LONG OVERLAND JOURNEY TO VIKINGSHOLM AND HE IS WELCOMED AT EVERY STEAD AND STRONGHOLD, FOR A SKALD HOLDS MUCH HONOR AMONG THE WINTER-BOUND VIKINGS

2-28 1464

THE FAR-WANDERING VIKINGS LISTEN TO THE WILD MUSIC AND DREAM OF ADVENTURE AND STRANGE NEW LANDS TO RAID. AFTER A PAUSE THE SKALD AGAIN PLUCKS THE STRINGS AND SINGS THE LAST VERSE CALLED 'THE CHALLENGE AND THE FULFILLING'. THEN HE TELLS OF THE KING'S REWARD, OF THE GOLD AND FURS TO BE HAD BY ALL WHO DARE THE VOYAGE.

NEXT WEEK— **The Workshop**